The Sugar Demons

Johnathan Cranford

For Sonya and Ariel

Contents

Introduction
An Addicts Guide to Conquering Sugar Addiction

Congratulations on discovering the book that will help you finally end the vicious cycle of relapses in your struggle with sugar addiction. As you've likely discovered, most of the advice in books and articles about sugar addiction is only marginally useful. "Drink more water and eat healthy food? Thanks Internet! That should really help when I'm dead tired from work, the kids are screaming, and all I can think about is ice cream." What you need are real strategies to get through sugar withdrawal and into the "promised land" where sugar cravings are nonexistent, energy is high, and weight loss is effortless.

Inside you'll find:

- A science based (addict approved) step by step plan for conquering your addiction to sugar and refined carbohydrates.
- A serious approach that treats addiction like the war that it is while also turning it into a fun game you can win.
- How to take "discipline" and "willpower" out of the equation in your battle with addiction.
- A list of supplements that will give you an edge against the Sugar Demons.
- Real world stories and experiences from the life of an actual sugar addict.

- How to take the hassle out of meal prep and how to get all of your meals prepped for the week in under an hour.
- Worksheets to keep you on track as you work through this process.

Chapter 1
The Sugar Demons

7p.m. Central Standard Time, just after dinner.

Taco-seasoned ground turkey, sweet potato, a few cups of steamed broccoli; the perfect recovery meal after a long work day and a hard workout in the gym. But before I can sleep, there's one more trial to overcome. A final challenge from an enemy I know too well. It's the nightly assault of the Sugar Demons.

I've fought this battle countless times before. If I can resist their temptations, I'll sleep soundly, wake up refreshed, and tomorrow gets a little easier. But if I lose there are consequences. I wake up feeling tired, head unclear, my body struggling to get out of bed. Worst of all, the Sugar Demons get stronger and harder to resist.

If I continue losing, I risk falling into a death spiral of weight gain and depression. The sugar leads to weight gain, the weight gain leads to depression, and the demons feed on depression. In turn this leads to binge after binge, more weight gain, more bad feelings and so on and so forth. This pattern must be avoided at all costs.

But they whisper…

Not with words mind you. My demons communicate through feelings.

It makes them hard to detect and harder to kill. They shine a spotlight on your negative emotions and suggest a solution in the most friendly, casual, innocent way. But the solution is always the same, always sinister.

"*You are stressed.*" they whisper.

Stress is their favorite weapon. It's the one I'm most likely to cave to; although, "bored" works well enough on occasion. You recognize the feeling and know what you need to do to make it go away, at least for a little while. A pint of ice cream would be my go-to delivery mechanism. I learned long ago not to keep any in the house. Sugar is a drug and when the drug is that close, the battle is already lost. Ridding your house of sugar is the first strike against the demons in what is to be a very long war.

But the enemy is patient. They have other ways of getting to you.

Their next trick will be allowing you to think sugar itself is the enemy. It is not. Sugar is just a series of atoms linked together, mostly carbon and hydrogen. Hence the term "carbohydrate". *Sugar* is just a chemical fact. *Sugar Demons* on the other hand are destructive creatures who hide in your subconscious. In other words, you carry them with you. You carry them with you in the same place a heroin junkie carries his demons. Though sometimes I envy the heroin junkie. At least every friend, family member, coworker, TV commercial, sign, and billboard isn't trying to feed *his* addiction. Is it not heresy to refuse a slice of cake at a your nieces' birthday party? My demons are enabled by an entire culture.

So you empty your pantry of all sweets and you swear off desserts. Your efforts work, for a time. The demons' hold upon you weakens. They get smaller, quieter. But they wait. The enemy is patient. It waits until you sort of forget that sugar lives in bread and pasta and alcohol and other processed foods. It waits for you to forget your triggers. It waits for you to think it's finally gone.

But they whisper…

"*You are stressed.*"

You know this trick. You're capable of avoiding anything resembling a dessert. You've trained for this. You are stronger now. But you happen to be driving near a barbecue restaurant and realize you could totally go for some ribs right now. That will make you feel better. And ribs are protein, so technically it's not cheating right? As you head home, still licking the barbecue sauce from your fingers, you feel as though you've made a decent compromise, but the Sugar Demons are feasting on the deceptively sugary sauce.

The next day, your defenses are down thanks to the choice you made yesterday. This time you have a sandwich, not even giving consideration to the fact that the refined carbohydrates in bread are basically just sugar. Later, you compromise again with tortilla chips and salsa from your favorite Mexican place. The day after that you give in once more with a fast food burger for the sake of convenience. As you continue to give in the demons grow in size and strength. The feelings they feed you are stronger, the impulse to indulge unshakable.

Finally, you end up grabbing a package of Oreo's during your weekly grocery. It falls into your cart with zero resistance. Once it's there you have second thoughts about it, but you're already rationalizing. The demons communicate with feelings, but the justifications are your own.

"I *know* I shouldn't eat this, but I'll get right back on track tomorrow."

Five days later, you're sitting in front of the TV eating a pint of Haagen Das with another back-up pint in the freezer.

"You're pathetic."

That's your own voice. The demons don't taunt. They're far too sophisticated for that. They would never lower themselves to insults. But this kind of self-talk can easily take you down a dark path, where the demons lead and you always follow.

You learn you can never compromise with this enemy. You learn it the hard way.

But you're a fighter. So you get back to meal prepping. You get back on a schedule. You resolve to fight harder this time. You keep busy because you've heard the saying about idle hands. But *they* know eventually a weekend will come where you have nothing planned. Nothing to occupy your time.

The attack will come on a day when your healthy meals are already prepared in neat little Tupperware containers. There is no junk food in the house. The battle is in your favor.

But they whisper,

"*You are bored.*"

With a long day of Netflix in front of you, you think, "Maybe I should grab some trail mix or something while I watch TV." That small compromise is enough to put you back on the slippery slope to overindulgence. By the afternoon you will have progressed to potato chips, and, from there, probably cookies.

You learn "boredom" is just another ambush to watch out for.

So you start over. You begin the fight again. Your resolve is stronger this time. You know yourself better. You know that if you keep to a regular schedule, work, go to the gym and eat meals at regular times everyday, then it becomes easy to avoid the demons. Monday through Friday are a breeze, and when you keep busy on weekends, avoiding the demons becomes effortless. You keep to this pattern for a few weeks and are once again in control.

It feels amazing.

The demons cannot stand against you when you're strong like this. So they wait. They wait for a gap in your defenses. Inevitably you give them one, because life is not meant to be lived on a schedule all the time. You take a vacation or you come down with a head cold or some social engagement breaks your pattern, leaving you without the time or the energy to meal prep.

Your successes over the past few weeks have made you stronger, but they have also made you arrogant. You think that if you give in, just for one day, just for the sake of convenience, you can get right back on track the next. Because you've got this. You are in control now.

But they whisper,

"You deserve a break."

One day turns into six. Getting back on track the next day is never a given. You learn this lesson over and over again. You learn that anything interrupting your schedule, anything that breaks your pattern of behavior leaves you vulnerable to the enemy. Vacations are especially problematic. Most importantly you learn that you are never as in control as you think you are. As they say in Alcoholics Anonymous, "you are powerless over this."

Over time, you realize the Sugar Demons have patterns as well. They were born of patterns. Before you were old enough to speak your parents rewarded good behavior with candy and other sugary treats. They gave you ice cream to cheer you up when you were sad. Every birthday into adulthood was celebrated with cake. Every accomplishment, every great milestone in your life, was celebrated with sugar. Every tragedy was consoled by it. The pattern is simple: Need a reward? Have some sugar. Feeling a bit down? Have some sugar.

The reward center of your brain is directly linked to your emotional dependence on sugar, and the Sugar Demons have a direct line on your emotions. So you know that when you're feeling sad, elated, bored, or stressed, the demons will come. That's the predictable part of the disease.

You cannot fight them with logic. Otherwise, you could just say, "This is bad for me so, I'm gonna turn it off." Obviously, this has no effect on the demons except perhaps to amuse them. But knowing when and how they will strike is valuable. With this knowledge you can form your own patterns, which allow you to resist. Keep sugar out of the house, never compromise, stick to a schedule, stay active; these are your weapons. And for God's sake, keep learning how they fight. It's your *only* chance.

So after I finish dinner, I prepare for the inevitable showdown. The demons love to come at this time of night. They tell me I'm stressed. It's usually over something work related, something that must get done tomorrow or else. It's a hollow feeling, like I'm empty even though I just ate.

I've been here so many times now. I know how to resist. I know how to win this fight. I *will* win this fight.

But they whisper…

Sound Familiar?

If any of this sounds familiar to you, then you are dealing with sugar addiction, or as I like to call it; the Sugar Demons. Their victims are everywhere. In fact, just by being an adult over the age of twenty, there's a pretty good chance you're either addicted to sugar or have a poor relationship with it. It's far more common than you might think. While nobody has an exact number of how many people are currently suffering from sugar addiction, a good place to start is by looking at obesity rates.

The current obesity rate in the U.S. is over thirty-six percent according to CDC data. We can assume the majority of those people are sugar addicted for reasons I will outline in another chapter. An additional thirty-three percent of adults are not yet obese, but are considered overweight. These numbers add up to nearly seventy percent of the adult population! However, not every person who is overweight is sugar addicted, and not every sugar addict is overweight, either. My guess is if we remove all of the overweight people who are not sugar addicted from the equation and add in the average or underweight people who are, then we would still arrive at a number somewhere in the vicinity of seventy percent. That's seven out of every ten people you know! Sure, that's only a rough estimate and likely inaccurate, but it's plausible. What if the real number is only six out of ten people or even five of ten? That's still at least *half* of everyone you know. Don't forget these numbers only account for overweight and obese adults, but sugar addiction often begins much sooner than adulthood.

An even better indicator of how many people are sugar addicts is the number of people suffering Type II Diabetes. According to the most recent CDC data, over one hundred million people are living with diabetes or have prediabetes. In other words, a full third of the U.S. population is living with a disease or the precursor to a disease caused by the overconsumption of carbohydrates like sugar and high fructose corn syrup. That's one out of every three people! If we take into account how many people become sugar addicted long before the precursors to Type II Diabetes appear (An A1C measurement of 5.7%-6.4% or a fasting blood glucose of 100mg/dl to 125mg/dl), then we're talking even more people. The point is you are not alone in this.

People everywhere are dealing with sugar addiction, but due to the fact our culture tends to reserve the word "addiction" for things like street drugs, many are not able to recognize their own sugar addiction for what it is. The earlier section you read about my own internal struggle with the Sugar Demons is actually from a blog post I wrote in 2016.

I still receive a good amount of feedback on that post from friends and strangers alike; people who want to tell me how much they identify with my experience. One Redditor commented, "It's like you're inside my brain!" More often though, people begin their comments with the qualifier "I don't think I have a sugar addiction but…" then proceed to tell me how they often experience feeling exactly what I describe in the post. They're sugar addicts who are just not comfortable associating themselves with the word "addiction." Consider yourself fortunate to be in the small minority of people who recognize they have a problem. This book is written for people like you.

How This Book Works.

Each chapter outlines a different strategy for fighting the Sugar Demons. I strongly recommend using all of my tactics as opposed to cherry-picking. Sugar Demons are formidable, so it's best to be over-prepared than to get caught with your pants down. They are trying to kill you after all.

In subsequent chapters, I will explain each strategy in detail and also tell you how I've applied it in my own life. Everyone's life is different, so it's up to you to choose how to apply these methods to your own situation. Don't worry though, all of these approaches are simple enough so anyone should be able to practice them. Most of this stuff is really about changing what takes place between your ears.

Each chapter will end with a nutritional-supplement strategy as a bonus. It's not necessary to use any of the nutritional supplements recommended in order to successfully battle your Sugar Demons, but I've found them to make the process a little easier.

Now let's talk about the enemy.

Sugar vs. Sugar Demons

Sugar

Miriam-Webster defines sugar as:

> 1. A sweet crystalline substance obtained from various plants, especially sugar cane and sugar beet, consisting essentially of sucrose, and used as a sweetener in food and drink.

> 2. Any class of soluble, crystalline, typically sweet tasting carbohydrates found in living tissues and exemplified by glucose and sucrose.

> 3. Used as a term of endearment. "Whats wrong, sugar?"

As an addict, I never think of sugar as "a sweet crystalline substance." In the grips of a craving, it's a mental picture of cookies, paired with a vague sense of how they might taste, and a feeling that pushes me toward eating them. But before I succumb to eating blatantly sweet foods like cookies, I'll often get started down the path with the non-sweet tasting carbohydrates such as a piece of bread, and, prior to that, maybe the sweet chemicals from a diet soft drink. Of the three things I just mentioned (cookies, bread, and diet soda), only one of them is made with what we think of as sugar, so for the purposes of this book we need to redefine what sugar is to us as addicts, and specifically what kinds of foods and ingredients to avoid.

Sugar is a carbohydrate so "carbohydrate addiction" is just another way of saying sugar addiction. Of course there are two different types of carbs, simple and complex. Sugar is a simple carb, it spikes blood sugar while complex carbs like whole wheat are supposed to be "better" for us because they elevate our blood sugar, slowly over a longer period of time. In the end though, all carbohydrates convert to glucose (sugar) in your body. Does it matter if it happens all at once or slowly throughout the day? Complex carbs are just the slow-release version of our drug.

I'm not saying all forms of carbohydrates are bad and we can never eat them again, but we need to understand "sugar" is anything that feeds our addiction which includes many forms of refined carbohydrate and artificial sweeteners. Refined carbohydrates, though not sweet, can be just as bad as sugar. I can binge on a box of saltine crackers just as easily as a tray of Oreo's. Technically, the artificial sweeteners in diet soda aren't carbohydrates, but they have a psychological effect on me which eventually leads to binging on actual sugar. Even the white potatoes in a potato salad can be problematic if I overindulge.

To keep all of this stuff straight, I've come up with a basic system for classifying the carbs I can eat, the carbs I can't eat, and the carbs that require caution. Consider a traffic light. Green means "go," eat as much as you want of these foods. Yellow means "Be cautious, very cautious." Foods in the yellow category can get me into trouble unless I consume them in small or measured portions. Red means "Stop!" I don't eat foods in the red category without suffering the consequences, and it may always be that way for me. Through trial and error, I've managed to put together a comprehensive list of carbohydrate containing foods in all three categories.

Green-Light Carbs

Any non-starchy vegetable including:

Broccoli
Asparagus
Green Beans
Cauliflower
Celery
Brussels Sprouts
Cabbage
Cucumber
Mushrooms
Peppers
Salad Greens (Lettuce, Spinach, Arugula)
Sprouts
Okra
Zucchini Squash

A few starchy vegetables including:

Sweet Potatoes
Beets
Winter Squash (Butternut, Acorn)

Yellow-Light Carbs

Starchy vegetables including:

White Potatoes
Red Potatoes
Fingerling Potatoes
Yukon Gold Potatoes
Carrots
Parsnips
Green Peas

Whole Wheat and Grains:

Corn
Whole Wheat Breads
Whole Wheat Pasta
Brown Rice
Oats
Rye
Barley

Beans and Legumes:

Black Beans
Red Beans
Kidney Beans
Lentils
Peanuts (yep, these are legumes)
Pinto Beans
Soy Beans

High Fat Dairy:

Cheese
Sour Cream
Heavy Cream

Note: High Fat Dairy products are low-carb foods and almost in the Green-Light category, but I put them in the Yellow-Light category because excessive consumption can be problematic for me.

Fruit:

Berries (blueberries, strawberries, blackberries, raspberries)
Apples
Bananas
Oranges
Pears
Melon (water, and cantaloupe)
Kiwi
Grapes
Cherries

Red-Light Carbs

Any foods with these added forms of sugar:

Table Sugar (sucrose)
HFC (High Fructose Corn Syrup)
Agave Nectar
Honey
Maple Syrup

Barley Malt

Beet Sugar

Molasses

Brown Rice Syrup

Cane Juice

Brown Sugar

Caramel

Coconut Sugar

Corn Syrup

Evaporated Cane Juice

Fructose

Galactose

Glucose

Fruit Juice Concentrate

Maltodextrin

Rice Bran Syrup and Rice Syrup

Sorghum Syrup

Turbinado Sugar

There are other names for added sugar but if you avoid processed foods you will avoid most of these.

Processed Wheat and Grains:

White Bread (all forms)

Pasta

Corn Bread

Corn Meal

White Rice

Oats (including oatmeal)

Fruit:

Fruit Juices (including anything you juice at home in a juicer)

Dairy:

Milk
Yogurt
Half and Half

Artificial Sweeteners:

Aspartame (Nutrasweet)
Erythritol
Saccharin (Sweet N Low, Equal)
Sorbitol
Sucralose (Splenda)
Xylitol

Alcohol in all of its forms, including beer, wine, and the hard stuff.

When I consume red-light carbs, it usually means I'm in the grips of a sugar binge or on my way to one, but yellow-light carbs can be part of my daily life as long as I'm careful. For instance, I eat six ounces of blueberries every day with breakfast. Blueberries are a nutrient rich super food I want to keep in my diet even though they're sweet and contain fructose. They're a "yellow-light" food because the sugar in natural, unprocessed foods like blueberries doesn't increase my cravings if I eat reasonable portions. So just to be safe, I measure out exactly six ounces of blueberries every morning on my food scale. That's how careful I am with yellow-light foods.

You'll notice I'm not prescribing a specific diet here. Everyone is free to feed themselves in a way that works best for their individual body. I don't care if you do this as a Vegan, a Paleo diet, a Zone Diet, or you count macros so long as you avoid eating red-light foods. I'm truly indifferent when it comes to what specific diet program you choose to follow. The main priority here is to get you off sugar.

Sugar is just a jumble of carbon, hydrogen, and oxygen atoms. It's neither alive nor dead. It's just a chemical compound similar to the air you breath and the water you drink. It may be your poison, but it's not your real enemy. Think about other poisons you have in your house. There's no invisible hand pushing you toward the cabinet below the kitchen sink to stare at the bottles of Lysol and Windex the way you stand in front of your refrigerator staring at the ice cream. The real enemy is the thing you can't describe. It's the internal force guiding you to the refrigerator; the empty feeling, the drumbeat in the back of your mind that won't go away until it gets what it wants. Let's meet that enemy now.

Sugar Demons

Indulge me for a moment while I use a short story from my experience as a public school teacher to help me explain where Sugar Demons come from:

The sixteen-year-old lies on the floor refusing to get up. I look up at the clock and make a note that he's been lying on the floor for twenty minutes now. I ask him for the fifth time if he's ready to return to his desk and get on task. He responds with profanity. He takes off one of his shoes. He examines his shoe for a while, then proceeds to throw it up in the air and play catch with himself. I continue to document his behavior.

As a public school teacher who works exclusively with emotionally disturbed children, this isn't anything I haven't seen before, but it's not how I want to spend seventh period, my last class of the day.

The student is roughly my size. If he does anything that constitutes a danger to himself or the other people in the room, it's my job to physically restrain him. Right now it seems like his behavior might escalate in that direction. The situation has me on edge. I can't afford to let my guard down in case he does something sudden-like pick up a desk and throw it or try to stab me with a pencil. In other words, I have to stay alert.

It's a low to medium level of stress that doesn't go away until the dismissal bell rings. By some miracle, we manage to make it through the class without incident. The stress doesn't completely go away though. It transforms into a tired feeling. All I want to do is go home and turn my brain off.

The problem with turning your brain off is that you can't. It would kill you. What you can do is turn off parts of your brain that think about and reflect on experiences you'd rather forget. Many people do it everyday. Most do it in front of a TV screen or a cell phone.

When I get home from my stressful day, I sit down in front of the TV and turn off the thinking part of my brain. It's time to binge watch something good on Netflix. At some point, I get up and wander to the pantry. It's a reflex. I don't even realize I'm doing it until I find myself standing in the pantry door looking over my options. We don't keep junk food in the house on account of my addiction, so fortunately I don't see any cookies. It occurs to me that even by standing there I'm asking for trouble, but an invisible hand is holding me in place, guiding me to find something.

I spot a jar of my wife's peanut butter. Telling myself I'll just have one or two tablespoons, I bring the jar back to the couch and sit down. The thinking part of my brain shuts off again. I eat the whole jar of peanut butter before even finishing the first episode of "Stranger Things".

Let the self-loathing begin.

Fight or Flight

The part of your brain that stays active all the time (including while you sleep) is called the Limbic System. It's often referred to as the "lizard brain," because if you take away the higher levels of the brain, what you're left with is basically the same as what a lizard has for brains. The Limbic System manages primal, emotional responses such as fear and anger, it tells your adrenal glands to start pumping in the face of danger, and it rewards biological behaviors such as sex and eating via the release of the neurotransmitter dopamine. Basically, the Limbic System is all the brain you need if your life revolves around eating, not getting eaten by predators, and reproducing.

It's powerful enough to override the other "thinking" parts of your brain. The Limbic System is the part of your brain the Sugar Demons have taken over. It's where they live. All activity in the Limbic System takes place below the level of conscious thought, and that's why logic and reason don't work against the Sugar Demons. It's the reason you open a bag of cookies, while simultaneously thinking, "STOP! Why am I doing this?" It's why you sometimes feel helpless.

Let's go back to my seventh period class for a moment to look at what my Limbic System is up to. While observing the student lying on the floor becoming increasingly belligerent towards me, I realize there's a good chance he might become physically aggressive at any moment. My Limbic System recognizes the danger and, being responsible for the fight or flight response, orders a hormone cocktail in the form of adrenaline and cortisol to prepare my body to deal with the threat. This hormonal reaction is the biological definition of "stress" and it doesn't require an extreme situation like the one I'm describing to trigger it. In fact, it happens to all of us almost every day. Bad traffic or a hectic work day can just as easily cause your Limbic System to react the same way mine does when facing a potential physical threat. Nothing bad has to actually happen, it's the possibility of something bad happening that causes stress. Just to give some perspective, I have the same stress response when I think I'm going to be late for a movie.

The Sugar Demons are hanging out in your Limbic System just waiting for this stress response to happen. It opens a door for them. The stress response evolved to help you survive dangerous situations. In extreme situations, it can give you superhuman strength and pain tolerance, but it comes at a cost. The release of adrenaline and cortisol is not easy on your body. It leaves you feeling… well, stressed!

Whether it's an acute response to an extreme situation like being chased by a bear or the slow drip of stress hormones you get from a busy work day, the result is the same; physical and mental exhaustion. The Sugar

Demons recognize this and immediately begin working on the other side of your Limbic System, the part that's responsible for rewarding your behaviors.

Your Reward System

As stated earlier the Limbic System is also responsible for rewarding certain behaviors (like sex and eating) with the neurotransmitter dopamine. Dopamine is a "feel good" hormone that releases in response to doing something beneficial to survival like eating life-sustaining food. This part of the brain most likely evolved to help us keep doing the things which allow us to survive long enough to produce offspring and care for them. Remember that lizards have all this stuff, too. In fact, it's all they have. Chasing the dopamine reward is the reason they keep eating bugs and making baby lizards.

Just like lizards, we're chasing the dopamine reward, too, but only when our Limbic System has been hijacked by Sugar Demons do our brains think sugar is worth a greater amount of "reward" (dopamine) than the healthy foods we should be eating.

Even without the help of the Sugar Demons, sugary foods already elicit a greater dopamine response than healthy foods for two reasons.

The first reason is simply that sweet foods cause a greater dopamine response than bland foods. This is well documented, and we'll delve into why this is in a later chapter.

The second reason is your emotional connection to sugar. Emotional memory is another thing the Limbic System is responsible for. If I say the word "birthday," do you not immediately think of a cake with candles on top? For most of us sugar has been used to celebrate and reward behaviors our entire lives. Did your dad ever take you to get ice cream after winning a little league game or to reward you for sitting quietly in church? You have an emotional connection to sugar, because it's been used to mark so many happy occasions. So when you see Christmas cookies and immediately get that same feeling you had as a child, you can thank your Limbic System for consolidating that emotional memory.

These processes take place in the parts of your mind you can't see. So when you get up to get a glass of water only to find yourself standing in the pantry with no memory of consciously choosing to do so, it's probably because you didn't. The explanation for why it happens is simple: You feel stressed from any one of the thousands of stress causing things in modern life. It would be nice if the feeling would go away. Subconsciously, you know eating foods containing sugar will reward you with a dopamine response, which relieves some of the stress. The more of it you eat, the more dopamine you get. The more often you do this, the less resilient you are to dealing with stress in a healthy way. The cycle repeats over and over again.

To my best understanding, Sugar Demons are a dysregulation occurring in the limbic system between your stress response and your reward response. But it helps me to think of them as actual demons who are trying to enslave and kill me. I don't want to be a slave to this cycle anymore. I want to kill my Sugar Demons. I want to fight them and be the hero of my own story. In the next chapter, I begin to tell the story of how I fight the Sugar Demons and the strategies I use to successfully defeat them.

This first chapter is a little heavy on all the reasons why this is going to be an uphill battle, but I'd like to end on something hopeful. The good news is, once you get through those first ten days or so, you enter what I call "the promised land". The promised land is awesome because that's where sugar cravings occur with less frequency and are totally mild compared to the cravings you're used to experiencing now. Once you reach the promised land, staying off sugar is a breeze. The first four chapters of this book contain tips and strategies to get you through your first ten to fourteen days sugar free. So have hope! The promised land is only about a week or so away.

In the meantime, your first task is to be cognizant of when you are having sugar cravings. You'll be surprised to find out how regular and predictable they are once you start paying attention. For me, they usually come right after I get home from work, and again after dinner. Everyone is different, so just start keeping track of what times of day and what kind of events trigger a craving. It won't take long for you to see the pattern. At the end of chapter two, there's an incredible supplement strategy that works wonders for me, but you won't be able to take advantage of it unless you start figuring out the pattern of your cravings now.

Chapter One Cheat Sheet

- For the purposes of this book, the term "sugar" encompasses all forms of processed carbohydrate, alcohol, and artificial sweeteners with the exception of Stevia.
- Stick to green light carbs for the first ten days or until you reach the "Promised Land" where cravings become tolerable and less frequent.
- After you reach the "Promised Land" you may start adding in some yellow light foods in small, measured quantities.
- Sugar, and other processed foods hijack the limbic system by causing a greater release of the neurotransmitter dopamine than other healthier foods.
- **Start tracking your cravings NOW. A pattern will emerge, giving you insight as to when and where your Sugar Demons will assault you with cravings.**

Chapter 2
Get Superbetter than Your Demons

What the heck is Superbetter?

Sometime around my thirty-eighth birthday, two things happened which allowed me to start battling my Sugar Demons successfully. The first was, after many failed attempts over the years to reign them in, I finally realized I wasn't good enough to beat the sugar demons on my own. The second was discovering the book *Superbetter* by Jane McGonigal.

Most people discover Jane McGonigal through her TED Talks, I first learned of her when she was a guest on my favorite podcast, The Joe Rogan Experience. Something about her story captivates me. Jane is the first person to earn a PhD studying the psychology of gamers and is herself a video game designer. After suffering a severe concussion with persistent post concussion syndrome in 2009, she devised a game to help her heal. *Superbetter*, has seven rules which can be applied to almost any *real life* challenge:

1. Challenge yourself.

2. Collect and activate power-ups.

3. Find and battle the bad guys.

4. Seek out and complete quests.

5. Recruit your allies.

6. Adopt a secret identity.

7. Go for an epic win.(1[1])

While I highly recommend reading the book *Superbetter* to anyone facing any sort of challenge or difficulty in life, in this chapter I'll describe how I apply the rules of Superbetter in my own life to fight the Sugar Demons so you can do the same. Use the techniques in this chapter as a foundation to build upon the tools and strategies outlined in later chapters. Think of it as a system of combat designed exclusively for fighting Sugar Demons. Trust me, you *need* a system.

Since rules one and three are redundant in my case, I have fewer rules for playing Superbetter and they are ordered a bit differently. This is just a matter of preference on my part. The less rules to keep track of the better.

The first rule, "Challenge Yourself," requires no explanation. You already know what the challenge is. You want to be free of sugar addiction. You want to stop being a slave to your cravings for sweet and processed foods. You want to end the thirst for foods that rob you of energy; foods that damage your body; foods that make you fat; foods that have taken the lives of people you know and so many more you will never meet. You want to kill your Sugar Demons. Challenge

---

[1] Jane McDonigal, *Superbetter* (New York: Penguin, 2015) 23.

accepted.

The third rule, "Find and Battle the Bad Guys", can also be eliminated in this case as we already know who the "bad guys" are. The "bad guys" are obviously the Sugar Demons and we don't need to find them, because they will find us. We do need to fight them however, so let's get to how I do it. Here are my rules for Superbetter as it applies to fighting the Sugar Demons:

1. **Adopt a secret identity.**

2. **Activate at least three power-ups per day.**

3. **Complete at least one quest per day.**

4. **Recruit at least one ally.**

5. **Define your "Epic Win".**

Five rules are easier to keep track of than seven. Here's even more good news, you really only need to worry about the first three on a daily basis.

Turning your battle with sugar addiction into a game might seem silly at first, but remember, everything you've tried up to this point hasn't been enough to conquer your Sugar Demons. Fighting sugar addiction is serious business, but it can be also be fun. Superbetter is a game after all, so try to have a sense of humor about it and enjoy the process. Just remember the consequences of losing are blindness and having your limbs cut off.

Think I'm being overly dramatic? Just Google "symptoms of advanced Type II Diabetes".

There are worse ways to die, but not many. Follow the rules to the best of your abilities and you should be able to avoid this fate, even if you make some mistakes along the way.

Adopt a Secret Identity

"I'm not good enough."

The thought comes out of my mouth before I can stop it.

"Huh?" my wife responds.

"Oh, sorry, I was just thinking about my chances of winning the CrossFit Games this year."

"Well, you're right about that much," she says laughing, then kisses me sweetly.

A few hours later, we board a flight for Croatia. It's the vacation we've been looking forward to all year. While I may have masterfully concealed my true thoughts from my wife, I still have this feeling in my stomach like I just lost my entire paycheck in a poker game. What I really meant by "I'm not good enough" is "I'm not good enough to beat the Sugar Demons." It's the first time I can openly admit it to myself.

This new self-knowledge is depressing and a little scary. I begin focusing on all the reasons I can't control my sugar addiction. Lack of willpower. Not organized enough. Like to eat when stressed. Eat when bored. Hectic schedule. Not enough time to cook.

In essence, I begin to focus on all my weaknesses. This does exactly nothing to improve my situation or my mood. Fortunately, while relaxing on the beach in Dubrovnik listening to my favorite podcast, I learn about Jane McGonigal and her book *Superbetter*. Something about the way she describes becoming Jane the Concussion Slayer to help her survive post-concussion syndrome speaks to me. It's something I can use against my Sugar Demons! I immediately go to Amazon.com and one-click purchase the book. Once again, I have hope.

After reading *Superbetter* I realize that I'm absolutely right. I'm not good enough. I need to become something else. What hero, legend, book, or movie character could I become who possesses the qualities I require to defeat my Sugar Demons? Well, I've always loved the Star Wars universe since I was kid. The image of Mark Hamill wearing his black Jedi robes while calmly facing down his enemies keeps popping into my head. A Jedi master would be perfect for fighting Sugar Demons! They're brave, wise, disciplined, and they have incredible self control, both physically and mentally. Thus I begin thinking of myself as Jedi Master Johnathan. This is not something I'm eager to share with my friends.

Thinking of myself as Jedi Master Johnathan accomplishes two things. First, it forces me to focus on my strengths (or the strengths I want to have) rather than my weaknesses. Second, it gives me some distance from my problems. This *self-distancing* is a topic covered in *Superbetter*, and I believe it to be one of the most psychologically powerful weapons against the Sugar Demons. It sounds silly to me at first. Coming up with an idealized version of myself, trying to imagine what he would do in my situation. Then I have a sugar craving.

Instead of trying to resist it or just give in as usual, I ask myself, "What would Jedi Master Johnathan do?" The mental image of my Jedi self eating a bunch of donuts seems ridiculous. Eating donuts no longer correlates with how I see myself, so the craving passes. I just killed my first Sugar Demon. Dead. Murdered.

When you imagine the stress, the bad interaction at work, or the craving happening to your secret identity self instead of focusing on how it makes you feel, it gives you distance from the problem. That distance can often be enough to overcome the craving or give you the perspective you need in order to overcome whatever issue you're facing, so it doesn't turn into a sugar craving later. It also has the added benefit of enhancing willpower. While I don't think willpower is a reliable weapon against the sugar demons (more on why that is later), I do believe you need a small amount of it in order to start fighting back.

So before you move on, choose a secret, Sugar Demon slaying identity. Your character can be anything you like so long as it possess the strengths you need to fight the Sugar Demons. You do not need to share this identity with the public unless you choose to. In fact, I recommend you don't unless you enjoy making other people laugh at your expense. Then practice, practice, practice thinking of your secret identity self experiencing the same challenges you face in real time. Whether it's a strong sugar craving, the urge to skip going to the gym after work, or someone cutting you off in traffic, think to yourself, "What would *insert secret identity name here* do?"

This technique alone might be enough to help you kill your first sugar demon. Hopefully, the first of many. Want to really have fun with it? Keep track of every Sugar Demon you slay. If you're a data geek, do it on a spreadsheet, so you can track dates and times. You're almost guaranteed to find a pattern. If you're more artistically inclined, draw a picture of your secret identity and celebrate every victory by adding a mark for every demon you slay.

Activate at Least Three Power Ups Per Day

The Sugar Demons used to only come at night-right after dinner like clockwork. Then, work got a little more stressful, and, around that same time, we adopted a rambunctious new dog, so home got a little more stressful, too. Now, they come right after I get home from work. Just knowing when a sugar craving is coming is useful because you can mentally prepare yourself, but it's not always enough. I have to give myself the best possible chance to win every time I face my Sugar Demons, since the cost of losing is high. So as soon as I get home, before they begin their attack, I activate a power up.

Power ups are meant to give you a quick boost of positive emotion, which translates to *resilience.* Resilience is your ability to deal with any situation life throws at you. Resilient people are capable of bouncing back even after suffering terrible physical and emotional trauma from things like car accidents or divorce. When people who are not resilient suffer these same circumstances, they tend to get stuck in a cycle of negative emotions and take much longer to recover-if they recover at all. The good news is you can build up your own resilience every day by using power ups.

In the video game Super Mario Brothers, Mario eats mushroom power-ups to make him larger and more powerful. Think of power ups in life as working the same way they do in video games. Pac-Man can eat a power pellet, which makes him invincible and capable of killing the ghosts who are attacking him. Power ups in real life allow you to kill your Sugar Demons when they're attacking you. When you learn to time your power ups correctly, you will kill Sugar Demons before they even have a chance to attack.

A power up is anything that gives you a quick rush of positive feelings and can be reliably repeated. They fall into three categories; physical, emotional, and social.

A physical power up can be anything physical like going to the gym or knocking out a set of sit ups next to your desk at work. It doesn't have to be physically strenuous. Going for a walk around the block or just drinking a glass of water can work, too.

Emotional power ups are things like watching cute animal videos on YouTube or listening to uplifting music.

Social power ups give you a positive feeling from connecting with other people. High-fiving a coworker or texting some words of encouragement to a friend are examples of social power ups.

Activating power ups throughout the day is extremely powerful. It's crucial that you make a list of ten to fifteen power ups and commit to activating at least three per day. Pay attention to things that give you a positive feeling so you can add them to your list of power ups. Experiment with them as much as possible to find out what works best for you. I personally find that physical and social power ups work better for me than emotional power ups when dealing with Sugar Demons.

Curious about what power up I use to stop the sugar demons from coming at me right after work? I drink a glass of water with five grams of L-Glutamine mixed in. You'll notice L-Glutamine is the supplement strategy at the end of this chapter. That's right, supplements can double as power ups!

Here's a sample of my daily power up schedule:

6:30AM Physical Power Up: Stretch for two minutes.

6:45AM Emotional Power Up: Hug all three of my dogs before going to work.

11:00AM Social Power Up: High five a coworker or a student.

2:30PM Physical Power Up: Drink a glass of water with five grams of L-Glutamine mixed in.

4:00PM Physical Power Up: Go to the gym.

The efficacy comes from consciously doing something about your addiction everyday, even if it's something small, to make yourself a little stronger, a little harder for the Sugar Demons to pin down. The more you practice the stronger you'll become until the sugar demons are nothing but a tiny, distant voice, easily dismissed to the back of your mind. In the next section, we'll talk about another way you can gain strength every day, by completing quests.

Complete at Least One Quest Per Day

Upon returning from my vacation, where I was not even trying to fight my Sugar Demons, I decided it was time to put into practice the rules of *Superbetter*. The first quest I gave myself was to make a list of power ups. The second was to come up with more quests. I made an ordered list of very small, very achievable tasks I could complete that would each get me one step closer to being free of sugar addiction and gave myself permission to get through them at my own pace. Some days I completed lots of quests, while other days I only finished one. The only rule was I had to complete at least one per day.

Most of my quests could be completed in less than ten minutes. "Get rid of all the sugar and processed food in the house" was an early quest, as was "Research an easy to prepare healthy lunch you can bring to work with you." Later I graduated to more advanced quests like "Buy a lunch box today" and "Get to bed at least eight hours before you have to wake up." The quests were simple enough that I never failed to complete at least one every day. I learned quickly that even if everything else went wrong that day, I could still feel accomplished for the small amount of progress I made. Moving forward in life, no mater how small the progression, can empower you to get through anything.

If power ups are little boosts to help you get through the day, then quests are the small daily missions you undertake to get closer to your goal of achieving total dominance over your Sugar Demons. It's a way to push back against the enemy instead of just trying to survive their attacks. According to Jane McGonical, quests are what psychologist call "pathways forward." Each quest you come up with or visible pathway forward gives you hope. Each quest you complete makes you stronger and more experienced, so you can better handle the next one and the one after that and so on.

Chapter six is a series of worksheets, each one a quest, in chronological order so you can take an organized approach to combating your Sugar Demons. I've done the difficult part of organizing your plan of attack, but you're welcome to modify it if necessary. Feel free to go through them at your own pace as I did.

It's also a good idea to come up with a few quests of your own. Everyone's addiction is different, so it helps if you personalize your quests so they fit your life in a way that will maximize your success. Whatever you do, don't go to pieces if something happens to derail your progress or you go a day without completing a quest. Life has a way of doing that. Just get back on track the next day and keep moving forward. Quitting is not an option.

Congratulations! These first three rules are ninety percent of playing Superbetter to combat sugar addiction. The next two rules are just as important, but you won't have to manage them on a daily basis.

Recruit Allies

At my current age of forty, the thought of asking other people for help makes me cringe inside. It also doesn't help that I'm a dude. In my mind, guys who openly talk about their suffering are viewed as weak. It's not really true, but even in this progressive age, I can't seem to kill off the idea that talking to people about my emotional issues and asking for help just makes me look needy. It's a part of myself I'm still working on, but things are getting better.

When I was twenty-four, I lost a very close friend to suicide and blamed myself for failing to stop it. At the time, I was in school and working two part-time jobs, so I was too busy to really deal with what happened. Instead of talking about it, our group of friends went out, had a bunch of drinks, and went on with our lives. The oddest part was it didn't really hurt that much in those first few days after he died. The absence of pain is what bothered me most. But eventually the pain did come, and I continued being too busy to give it my attention. Thirteen years later the wound still wasn't healing. Then I sat down at my computer and wrote a blog post titled "Joseph Never Got Older" with tears streaming down my face.

At first, I was shy about sharing his story. It seemed way too personal, but I wanted to share my memory of Joseph so I clicked "post". The outpouring of love and understanding from friends and family who read it was incredible. It changed something inside me. The burden I'd been carrying for so many years suddenly got lighter. It didn't fix everything overnight, but it showed me how sharing my pain with others was the only way for me to become whole again. Also, nobody made fun of me or thought what I did was needy.

Sharing that post led me to write another post about sugar addiction titled "The Sugar Demons." You already read it in the first chapter of this book. A part of me must have realized if sharing my story about Joseph committing suicide could help me deal with that trauma, then sharing my struggle with sugar addiction might help me cope with it, too. The response to "The Sugar Demons" was even bigger. If anything it helped just to know so many people struggle with the same thing I do.

Playing Superbetter takes the stigma away from asking other people for help because you're not asking them for help, you're asking them to join in your game. Anyone can be your ally in Superbetter. You can ask them to come up with new quests for you or to brainstorm power ups. They can check in on you for weekly progress reports and help you celebrate your victories. You can even share your secret identity with them if you feel comfortable enough. Your allies can play as large or small a part in your game as you choose and you can have as many of them as you want. They don't even have to be people you've met in person. You can recruit online allies if that makes it easier; although, having an ally you can speak with in person tends to be more motivating.

You must not skip this step! Recruiting even one ally can be the difference between victory and permanent enslavement by your Sugar Demons. Any recovering alcoholic/drug user will tell you addiction isn't something you can beat on your own. You need allies. They help you stay accountable for your choices, give support when things are going poorly, and perhaps most important of all they are there when you need someone to just listen. Make it one of your early quests to recruit an ally.

Next up is the final rule of Superbetter. Congratulate yourself on making it to the last section of this chapter. There's a bonus for making it all the way to the end. At the end of this chapter you'll find our first supplement strategy, which doubles as a power up!

Define Your "Epic Win"

The first step of admitting to yourself you have a sugar addiction is a difficult place to get to. At the same time though, you feel hopeful you've identified the problem and can now take steps to overcome it. Don't be surprised if not everyone you talk to about this is supportive, including the people you love. People have a problem assigning the word "addiction" with something they may view as harmless. Also, they may be resistant to the idea because they're not be ready to see the damage sugar is doing in their own lives. Some people may just be afraid you'll change too much.

I remember an argument I had with my wife when I was still early on in the process of fighting my Sugar Demons. I had just achieved my first epic win by managing to make it through Thanksgiving and Christmas without eating a single dessert and was starting to feel back in control of my eating habits.

It started with me bragging in the kitchen of our home. "It's starting to get easier for me. I think I'm going to just keep doing this and not let sugar back into my life again."

"Never? Is that even realistic?"

Her answer comes in the form of a question, but her tone is borderline accusatory.

"I dunno, I hope so," I say.

"So you're never going to eat another dessert again?"

"I'm saying, I'm going to try not to. When I don't eat them, the cravings go away, and I'm sick and tired of having to fight the damn cravings."

At this point, I'm annoyed because it feels like she's being less than supportive.

Then she says "Ya, but I'm asking is that *realistic* to stop eating sugar long term?"

I start to raise my voice. "I DON'T KNOW, BUT I WANT TO TRY."

"Don't raise your voice at me, I'm just asking you a question."

Now I'm angry. She doesn't understand what's behind the question she's asking. Failure, that's what's behind it. A lifetime of struggling with my diet, poor health, and ultimately death at the hands of my Sugar Demons. Unless I get hit by a car or something first. The truth is, at that point I didn't know if I could beat this addiction long term and that scared me. My own fear and her not truly understanding what I was going through caused me to feel angry. We went to sleep not speaking to each other that night.

Of course, we made up the next day. In hindsight, "I'm through with desserts forever" is a bold statement to put on your loved ones. They might have a hard time accepting it at first, especially if they don't understand what you're going through. You may not be ready to accept it either depending on how much of a hold the Sugar Demons currently have on you. When I was in a cycle of eating sugar all the time, I couldn't imaging giving up cookies and ice cream forever, but after a few weeks of abstinence, I felt so good that the thought of giving those things up just didn't seem like much at all. In the end, desserts are just a form of mouth pleasure, and living your life for mouth pleasure isn't truly living.

Considering giving up sugar forever can be hard to accept for both you and the people around you, I suggest not making that your first "Epic

Win." It's better to start with something well-defined and measurable. "I will make it through the holidays without eating sugar" is a great example of an Epic Win for several reason.

First, it has a measurable time domain, roughly from Thanksgiving through New Years, the most difficult time for most people. Next, there's a high chance of failure. You can't call it an "Epic Win" if it's not sufficiently difficult. It should take some real fighting on your part to achieve. Finally, even if you do fail, you will have learned some lessons along the way to carry with you into the next battle. Not achieving your Epic Win shouldn't be the end of the world. When it happens, you spend a few minutes figuring out why you failed, how you can do better next time, and defining your next "Epic Win."

In the beginning, your Epic Win might be just to make it through a few days without eating sugar. That's okay as long as you keep raising the bar after each win. The more you practice playing Superbetter, the better you'll get. Even your failures can be victories as long as you learn from them. Just keep playing and keep wracking up wins. The Sugar Demons will be conquered in due time.

Supplement Strategy # 1

Welcome to the first supplement strategy. Remember, this part is no way mandatory. These supplement strategies are just meant to give you a slight edge in the game. That being said, they can be quite powerful. Also keep in mind we are all different and will respond in different ways to the things we choose to put into our bodies. Pay attention to your body's response to any new supplement you take, so you can make a determination as to it's efficacy. As always, it is important that you consult with a physician before you start taking any nutritional supplement.

Without further ado, here is your first supplement strategy:

L-Glutamine, Five grams per day taken with breakfast and before cravings.

When it comes to supplements, L-Glutamine is about as safe as they come. It's the most abundant amino acid in your blood stream and muscle tissue. Supplementing with it is widely regarded as safe. It's a substrate in so many chemical processes in your body that ingesting more of it can't really hurt you, but it can provide some interesting benefits. As an amino acid glutamine acts as a building block for muscle and various other tissues in the body. However, it is also critical in the creation of brain chemicals such as gamma aminobutyric acid (GABA) and gamma hydroxybutyrate (GHB). Both GABA and GHB have been proven in multiple studies to reduce the desire for sugar and alcohol in mice. Although there isn't much literature about L-Glutamine and sugar cravings in humans, a quick Google search for "L-Glutamine sugar cravings" will yield countless accounts from people who have successfully curbed cravings with regular supplementation.

I highly recommend trying this supplement for at least two weeks to see if it works for you. Since glutamine is used by the body for so many things, it's easy to get depleted. Personally, I take five grams a day in the morning after breakfast. Occasionally, I'll take another five grams in the afternoon if I find myself stressed or preoccupied with thoughts about eating something sweet. Once you figure out the patterns of your sugar cravings, this supplement becomes really powerful because you can take it right before the craving comes. Think of it as a will-power boost or a way to weaken a craving before it starts.

Additionally, L-Glutamine is quite beneficial to the health of your gut. It's the principal building block of your intestinal lining and the main source of fuel for it's cells.

Why is gut health relevant to sugar addiction? Well, your gut is responsible for the production of the neurotransmitter serotonin. Low levels of serotonin are thought to be a primary cause of depression. Certainly you've heard of drugs like Prozac or Zoloft for treating depression. These drugs (and numerous others like them) come from a class of drugs know as SSRIs. SSRI stands for Selective Serotonin Reuptake Inhibitor.

They work by slowing down the reabsorbtion of serotonin by your brain, thus ensuring your serotonin levels don't get too low. When the lining of your gut is weakened by stress, medications, poor diet, or illness, inflammation occurs. If it doesn't heal, it can begin to affect serotonin production. If serotonin levels drop too low it leads to depression. In a depressed state you're far more likely to give in to your Sugar Demons. An unhealthy gut can lead to an unhealthy brain so be good to your gut!

Chapter Two Cheat Sheet

- Superbetter is a game created by Author and Game Designer Jane McGonigal.
- The three rules you must follow every day are: Activate at least three power ups per day, complete at least one quest per day, and fight one bad guy every day.
- Define your "Epic Win" carefully. It should be difficult, yet achievable.
- **Use L-Glutamine to head off cravings before they start. This works best if you have already figured out the patterns of your cravings as assigned in Chapter 1.**

Chapter 3
Choosing the Battlefield

Discipline

"Every battle is won before it is ever fought."
-Sun Tzu from The Art of War

My friend Roberta used the term "disciplined" to describe me the other day. I thought to myself, "Disciplined? When did this happen?"

Growing up with ADHD no one ever complements you on your self control. In fact, "You lack discipline" is a phrase you get to hear all the time. Not just from parents, but teachers, coaches, and youth pastors, too. Even a few nuns back when I attended Catholic school would chastise me for lacking the discipline to practice my cursive handwriting.

On top of having ADHD, I was the kid who lost his jacket EVERY winter. I could never remember to bring a pen or pencil to school with me and I still can't stop biting my nails.

So when did I become this grand exemplification of discipline to others? To be clear, Roberta was referring to my uncanny ability to stick to my diet despite suffering from sugar addiction. It seems the ability to adhere to a diet is the cultural yardstick by which we measure a person's self discipline in adulthood. But I know better. The only way I've ever been capable of self discipline is to assume I don't have any.

If you operate under the assumption that trying to be disciplined is only going to lead you to failure, then you can start finding other means of achieving your goals. For example, if I go to work with my credit card but no lunch, my food choices come lunchtime are limited by my food environment. The food environment around my job is mostly fast food restaurants, a barbecue joint, and a Starbucks. When faced with that sort of food environment, the best I can do is go to the barbecue joint and order some grilled chicken with a side of green beans. But since I don't have any discipline to speak of, I'm much more likely to hit up the Whataburger drive-through. It requires a Herculean mental effort to force myself to drive to the BBQ joint and order chicken, whereas it requires no effort at all to pull into the drive-through. Like everything else in the universe, I almost always follow the path of least resistance. I know this about myself, so instead of testing my own self discipline by forcing a choice between boring chicken breast or a burger, I simply change my food environment.

Changing my food environment is simple, I always make sure to bring healthy food with me everywhere I go. Now my food environment includes an already-prepared delicious meal, which doesn't require me to leave the building. It would actually take more effort to go out and get something unhealthy, thus the path of least resistance is diverted to the healthy food I brought with me. Sure, I have to meal prep once or twice a week, but if you can't find one hour a week to meal prep then it's not a discipline issue, it's poor time management and possibly insufficient motivation.

There's nothing magical about what I do, and it certainly has nothing do with an abundance of discipline. It's just about realizing there are a million ways to fail your diet and only one way to succeed. You have to be prepared. You have to take "discipline" out of the equation. Those nuns may have been right about my lack of discipline, but they were dead wrong to place such emphasis on discipline as a precursor to success. What I lack in self discipline, I more than make up for in self knowledge and introspection. Which brings to mind another famous quote credited to the wise Chinese general Sun Tzu; **"Know yourself, know your enemy, and you shall win a hundred battles without loss."**

Forget Discipline

Discipline, willpower, self control. These are terms the processed food industry has been using for decades to shame us into thinking it's our fault for not being able to resist the highly processed, sugary foods they sell. All the while they've been adding more sugar and flavor chemicals to the foods they produce, thus making them more and more addictive. You've been fed these foods your entire life and they are being offered or advertised everywhere you go. No wonder you're addicted. Don't look to being disciplined or depending upon hidden reserves of willpower to miraculously get you out of this mess. It won't work. It hasn't worked.

Let's take discipline and willpower out of the equation for now. So what does that leave us to fight with? Information. We know when and where the enemy is going to attack. That is enough to turn the battle in our favor if we prepare for it. Think of your food environment as the battlefield. It's the landscape of possible foods you can choose to eat depending upon where you are and what time it is. Sugar cravings are the weapon the Sugar Demons will use against you to get you to choose the wrong food. Remember a craving for bread, pasta, or any of the other foods in the red and yellow light categories are simply well-disguised sugar cravings. If you choose one of these foods, the battle is lost.

The only way to win these battles consistently is by eliminating choice. Make it more difficult to "choose" wrongly than it is to choose wisely. You can do this by controlling the food environment within your home, and carrying your food environment with you when you leave home. Nothing is more powerful than this, and nothing in this book, or any other reputable book about diet, will work without it. Everything else is a fad, a scam, or just someone telling you what you want to hear.

Of course, you will have to do some cooking in order to achieve this. Don't panic! Even if you've never cooked a day in your life, I will walk you through the steps to prepare enough food to get you through the week in under an hour. That's correct, less than an hour per week is all it takes to change your food environment and turn the battle in your favor. Try to keep in mind that this is going to do more for you than just help you overcome sugar addiction. Once you get in the habit of preparing and eating healthy, food you'll start to feel healthier, look healthier, and probably save money, since you won't be relying on restaurants anymore.

Meal Prep in Under an Hour

Welcome to a typical day in the life of a superstar meal prepper! Sunday is my day to prep food for the week, but you can do it on whichever day works best for you. Make meal prep a Superbetter quest for the day you choose to cook. If you are lacking any kitchen equipment, such as Tupperware for food storage or a frying pan, then make it a quest to get those items one or two days before you tackle meal prep. While you're at it, grab a lunch box and some freezer inserts if you don't have those items. The lunch box is a critical piece of equipment for controlling your food environment, instead of it controlling you.

7:00 AM: Just waking up. It would be nice to sleep a little later, but the dog is licking my nostrils, so I wake up and let her out to pee, slowly realizing I need to do the same.

7:10 AM: Making scrambled eggs while defrosting six ounces of frozen blueberries in the microwave. This is breakfast. If I were only one or two weeks from quitting sugar, then I would skip the berries in favor of bacon or another healthy fat. Naturally occurring sugar in fruits like blueberries is only safe for me when my cravings are under control. In other words, they won't lead to stronger cravings later in the day.

7:20 AM: Eating breakfast.

7:30 AM: Playing with my dogs in the back yard.

8:00 AM: Heading out to the grocery store. This part is not included in the "hour" allotted to meal prepping and can be done on a different day, but I am including it because grocery shopping is technically part of the process. Also, it allows me to demonstrate how I navigate the grocery store in case you want to copy what I do down to the last detail.

8:07-8:40 AM: This may sound blasphemous to all the health nuts out there, but I skip the fresh fruits and vegetables section. Yup. I might stop to grab some avocados for extra fat or a couple sweet potatoes if I need extra carbs for heavy training days, but otherwise I just pass by the congested aisles of people squeezing cantaloupes and breathing on the apples. I buy the majority of my fruit and vegetables frozen. The reason I do this is because frozen vegetables are frozen the day they're picked. Often, the "fresh" vegetables you buy in a grocery store have been sitting in a warehouse for weeks or even months. Also, most frozen vegetables can be steamed in a microwave in five minutes, and you don't even have to take them out of the package. This completely eliminates the hassle of having to prepare vegetables on meal prep day.

My first shopping priority is protein. All of my meals consist of either a portion of protein and a healthy fat or a portion of protein and a safe carbohydrate like sweet potatoes. On most grocery days, I visit the meat section of the store and buy around three pounds of ground beef or ground turkey. Don't go any higher than eighty-five percent lean, unless you want the texture of your meat to mimic cardboard. I might pick up some steaks for dinner or some wild-caught fish, but for the purpose of this lesson, lets keep things simple. I'll also detail how to prep chicken breast and turkey patties if you prefer them to ground meat.

Next, I head over to the part of the store that sells nuts and pick up some dry-roasted almonds and cashews. These will be my fat source for most meals. They can be salted, but the only ingredients on the label should be the nut and some salt. If you buy fancy roasted or smoked nuts they tend to add some sort of unhealthy oil to the mix.

Then I'm off to the sparkling water aisle to stock up on La Croix, San Pellegrino, or Topo Chico. These are just brands of carbonated water I buy, because I enjoy the fizz. Regular water makes up the bulk of what

I drink, but I prefer to have sparkling water with meals. If you're past the cravings and into the "promised land," you can also try Zevia which is a Stevia-sweetened soda.

After that, I'm usually near the eggs so I put two or three dozen in my cart. I prefer to make scrambled eggs every morning, since it only takes a few minutes, but if you're one of those people who just doesn't have the time, I'll take you through how to prep breakfast along with lunch and dinner. I sometimes get a pound or two of bacon to go with the eggs or to use as a healthy fat source for other meals.

Finally, I'll visit the frozen section to pick up some frozen berries and a few bags of steamable broccoli and asparagus. If I'm out of staples like cooking oils or spices, I'll get those now. That's pretty much it for grocery shopping. Head to the check out aisle with the shortest line.

8:50 AM: Putting up Groceries.

9:00 AM: Meal prep actually begins. The first thing I do is preheat the oven to 400 degrees if I'm cooking sweet potatoes. Otherwise, I grab a large cooking pan (5-6 quarts), put it over medium heat on the stove top, and throw in a tablespoon of coconut oil. Once the oil is melted and coating the pan I throw in three pounds of ground turkey (or beef) and pour a packet of taco seasoning over it. Try to get packets of high-quality taco seasoning without additives, but it's not the end of the world if you use a taco seasoning that does. After it cooks for a minute or two, I'll start breaking up the ground meat with a spatula.

Once the oven is preheated, rinse off your sweet potatoes and put them in the oven on a large baking sheet. It's best if you line the baking sheet with aluminum foil for easy clean up after the potatoes are cooked. Sweet potatoes take a whole hour or so to cook, but you don't have to fuss over them while they're cooking. Once the sweet potatoes are in the oven, set your timer for an hour, and you can forget about them until they're done.

I continue stirring and breaking up the ground meat until it's fully browned. This only takes about fifteen minutes. Once it's done, I drain the excess fat out of the pan and transfer it to a large plastic storage container to be stored in the refrigerator. Then I wait for the sweet potatoes to finish cooking.

That's about all the effort I put into meal prep every week. I'll eat the ground turkey with a sweet potato or some nuts for lunch and do the same for dinner, unless I'm in the mood to cook steak or salmon.

I make breakfast fresh in the morning, but if you don't have time for that you can set a pot to boil a dozen eggs while you're cooking your meat. Eat the boiled eggs for breakfast with some avocado or bacon. In order to prep bacon you will have to use the oven and the baking sheet again. Set the oven to 400 degrees. While it's preheating, lay out the strips of bacon on the aluminum foil lined baking sheet. Cook the bacon for roughly twenty minutes depending on how crispy you like it. You can store the bacon in your refrigerator and reheat it in the microwave for breakfast to go with your eggs.

As you can see there isn't much to it. When you're done, you'll have sweet potatoes and three pounds of seasoned ground turkey that you can use as a base for both lunch and dinner. For a carb and protein meal, eat the ground turkey with one of the sweet potatoes. Remember you can spruce up the ground turkey however you like with salsa, chopped veggies, pico de gallo, or just eat it plain. For a protein plus fat meal, add a side of nuts or an avocado. Finally, round out each meal with a side of vegetables by tossing one of the bags of steamable frozen broccoli (or whatever microwave steamable vegetable you bought) in the microwave. I recommend eating a large serving of vegetables with each meal, but in reality I only do it for two out of my three meals per day.

To me, chicken breast gets boring really fast but if you prefer it to ground turkey or beef then just make sure to prepare it the way I'm about to show you so it doesn't come out dry and leathery.

First, you must brine your chicken! I know this sounds fancy to all you non-cooking types out there, but I promise it's really fast and easy. All you have to do is fill a large bowl with warm water and dissolve a handful of salt into it. Then, soak your chicken breasts in the bowl for a minimum of fifteen minutes.

Preheat the oven to 450° while you're waiting for the chicken to brine. Once the chicken is ready to come out of the brine make sure you have placed some paper towels on the plate to set the chicken breasts down on. Dry each chicken breast off with more paper towels.

Next, you'll want to rub each breast on both sides with olive oil or melted butter. This step adds flavor and helps to trap moisture in the meat. The last thing you want to do before putting your chicken in the oven is to rub them with salt and pepper or a spice mixture of your choosing. Finally, place the breasts on a roasting pan and put them in the oven for 15-18 minutes. Everyone's oven is different so you'll have to experiment a little to find the perfect baking time. When you remove your chicken from the oven, be sure to test it with a meat thermometer to ensure it has reached an internal temperature of 165 degrees Fahrenheit. If you skip this last step, you're risking Salmonella and possibly your life.

OK! There's one more easy prep I promised I would tell you about.

Turkey patties are possibly the quickest and easiest way to prep a lot of protein in a short amount of time. Hopefully you live near a grocery store that carries turkey patties. I use the Jenny-O brand from my local grocer. Turkey patties are super lean so make sure to enjoy them with a nice side of healthy fats like avocado or some nuts.

To cook patties, simply use the broiler option on your oven set to high. Salt and pepper both sides of each patty, place them on a roasting pan, and cook the patties for five to seven minutes on each side. Again, everyone's oven is a little different, so you'll have to figure out if you can get away with cooking the patties for five minutes per side or if they need the full seven minutes per side. You'll know after the first time how long they should cook. Turkey patties pair well with some mustard or salsa on them and they are so fast and easy to make!

The information in this chapter will make you a meal-prepping ninja inside of a week. Remember, the Internet is a great resource for any kind of "how to" question if you get stuck or want to prep something I've not discussed in this chapter. None of this is fancy with regard to cuisine, but it's functional and tastes good, which is the most important thing. If you're not enjoying the food you prep or you're getting tired of something, then switch to something else. The most important thing is that you actually like the food you're eating! If you have to force yourself to eat it, you won't last long on your diet.

Recently, I got tired of turkey patties after eating them almost every day for four months. When I switched to broiled pork ribeyes (prepared almost the same way as turkey patties), I actually got leaner, even though the pork ribeyes are fattier and more calorically dense!

There are no rules other than to stay consistent with your diet and don't let the Sugar Demons derail your progress.

Supplement Strategy #2

Today, after a gut-wrenching early morning cardio session, I followed my regular routine of taking two 500mg capsules of acetyl-L-carnitine. No big deal. This supplement has been around forever and doesn't really get much hype. The only reason I added it to my supplement stack in the first place is because Robb Wolf recommends it in his "My Training at 39" blog post, which happens to be exactly how old I am now. Then I showered and made breakfast.

After breakfast I, notice that the top shelf of the refrigerator, usually cluttered with various items, is almost completely bare. I haven't seen it this empty in a while. It looks naked. The reason for its current lack of clutter is that I've run out of groceries, and my Shipt shopper isn't due to deliver new ones for another two hours (in case you're not familiar, Shipt is an app I use sometimes to have my groceries delivered). Think of it as Uber for groceries. The time it saves me is worth the added expense. Sure, you pay a little more for your food and you have to tip, but you know what costs even more? Diabetes.

Think of it this way: Not having to shop for groceries eliminates an errand you would otherwise have to complete before meal prepping. Less errands frees up some time ensuring said meal prep actually gets done. If, after shopping for groceries and doing the one million other things you have to get done in a day, you're too tired to meal prep, then the Sugar Demons automatically win the next day when you make a terrible food choice, because you didn't have anything prepped. Lose enough battles to the Sugar Demons and you get Diabetes, which can cost you an arm and a leg, literally.

Still not convinced it's worth it? Think about all the dumb little "luxuries" we allow ourselves every day—designer coffees, overpriced glasses of wine, in-app purchases. We don't gain much from any of these things, but with Shipt you can spend money on something that actually buys you *more time*. Buying time is the wisest luxury-buy you can make, in my opinion. I don't always use it, but it definitely comes in handy on busy weekends.

Anyway, back to the refrigerator. With the top shelf clear I notice for the first time how dirty it is. The surface looks discolored in places. Little particles of food matter have settled into the creases along the borders of the shelf. Since nothing is currently occupying the shelf, I decide it would be easy to pull it out and wash it. First, I Google "what do I clean my refrigerator with?" According to marthastewart.com (no joke) warm water with dish soap works just fine. So I pull out the shelf and wash it.

Done.

But then I realize the rest of the fridge needs cleaning, too. So I start obsessively pulling out all the removable parts, including a shelf that was fastened in with screws, which requires me to find a screwdriver to complete the task. About 45 minutes later, the entire refrigerator is spotless.

That's what happens when you take acetyl-L-carnitine. You see what needs to get done and you just do it. Normally, I would've just done the easy part, cleaning the top shelf, and then hit the recliner for some Netflix. The acetyl-L-carnitine gives me the mental energy to get a lot more things done. It helps me write more, stay focused on tasks at work, and it gives me the mental fortitude I need to do the things that need to get done, so I can win against the Sugar Demons, even when I'm tired.

Acetly-L-Carnitine is the common amino acid L-Carnitine with an Acetyl group attached that allows it to cross the blood-brain barrier where it does some pretty amazing things. It has strong antioxidant properties, but what supplement doesn't? Seriously, whenever a supplement claims to be an antioxidant, I can't help but roll my eyes. Eat some blueberries, a few green veggies, maybe take a multivitamin, and you're already getting all the antioxidants you need. I don't take acetyl-L-carnitine for the antioxidant effect, but it's there, so I have to mention it.

More importantly, it directly contributes to acetylcholine production. Acetylcholine is a neurotransmitter, which helps us form and keep memories. In other words, it boosts your ability to remember stuff if you're deficient. In addition, it boosts two more neurotransmitters— Noradrenaline in the hippocampal formation, and Serotonin in the cortex. These two neurotransmitters are involved in mood and motivation. That's where the magic is in my opinion. I feel like getting more on my to-do list done when I take it.

After experimenting for the past six months with acetyl-L-carnitine, my final verdict is that it's awesome for people like me who run out of mental energy by mid-day. It basically does the opposite of what sugar does to my brain. I tend to cycle it for six weeks and then give myself a week or two, off the same way I would with caffeine. I haven't read that it's necessary to do this, but I like to give my body a break from any non-standard supplement just to be safe.

This stuff is dirt cheap, too. You can pick up a bottle of 200 capsules for around $20. I use the NOW Foods brand, but there are several reputable manufacturers.

Chapter Three Cheat Sheet

- Discipline and willpower are highly overrated when it comes to battling sugar addiction.
- Controlling your food environment is a more effective strategy than relying on willpower.
- **The only way to be in control of your food environment is to keep only safe foods in your home, meal prep weekly, and carry your meals with you when not at home. Any dietary advice to the contrary is either a fad or someone trying to sell you something useless.**
- Keep meal prep simple and easy so you don't skip it because you are overwhelmed by the task.
- Supplementing with acetyl-L-carnitine can give you the mental energy you need to meal prep or complete any other task/quest you set out to accomplish.

Chapter 4
Broccoli Angels

Before becoming a teacher, I worked in marketing for an insane asylum. Okay, we don't call them insane asylums anymore. Nowadays, we use the more politically correct term "behavioral health facilities." You wouldn't think a hospital for the mentally ill would even need a marketing department. It's not like those kinds of patients are browsing brochures and reading Yelp reviews before committing themselves, not most of them anyway. But the mentally ill were not my target audience. My job was to meet with the doctors and hospitals who send us their patients.

In Houston, there are only a handful of hospitals that specialize in treating mental illness. The more fortunate patients are funneled to one of these facilities. The less fortunate are sent to Ben Taub Hospital, locally known as Been Shot Hospital because it serves mainly poor people and gunshot victims.

Most of my work involved building relationships with local psychiatrists and their staff. I would bring lunch for the whole office, talk about our services, and educate them on what constitutes an "appropriate" patient for our facility. An "appropriate" patient is one that has insurance or some way to pay their hospital bill. If you did not meet that criteria, you were (behind closed doors, of course) deemed "inappropriate" for our facility. That's how it goes if you're a poor person suffering from mental illness. There are actually people who get paid to keep you from getting the care you need and send you to an already overburdened system at Ben Taub.

The intake office of a behavioral health facility is an even stronger deterrent for the uninsured. Pretend you're a doctor. I always picture myself as George Clooney from *ER,* but realistically I'm more like Zach Braff's character on *Scrubs.* Anyway, you have a patient who thinks aliens are controlling him. Normally, this isn't that big of a deal, except this guy thinks the aliens are controlling him through a microchip in his abdomen, and he keeps trying to cut it out with a hacksaw. Prime candidate for hospitalization. So you call the intake office of the hospital you wish to send him to. Most likely the person working in intake is going to tell you that they currently don't have any beds available, but if you send over the face sheet (a document that contains the patient's basic medical information, including insurance info) they will call you back as soon as something opens up. Whether or not something opens up often depends on the face sheet showing verifiable insurance information.

Sounds evil, but it's also necessary. There are a limited number of hospital beds for the mentally ill at any given time. I can recall multiple instances when there weren't any available mental health beds in the whole city. This happens pretty often, especially around Christmas. Also, a hospital is a business and subject to failing just like any other business. If the hospital takes on too many patients without the means to pay, then it bankrupts the hospital and suddenly there are even less beds to help the sick. I wish things were different, but that's the broken system we have.

The worst thing I witnessed by far, are the doctors who accept Medicaid. It's not the fault of the physician. They are doing the best they can to help the less fortunate. Unfortunately, the Medicaid reimbursement for treatment is so low, that the only way they can afford to provide services is by running a conveyor belt of patients through their office; one patient every fifteen minutes. This means you see your doctor for an extremely short amount of time before leaving with a prescription that alters your brain chemistry. The system is dangerously broken.

Working on the marketing side of behavioral health was like having a secret television channel that only shows you things other people don't want to see. I learned a great deal from it. One of my greatest teachers was a gentleman we will call Dr. Fowler. Dr. Fowler was the medical director of a major drug rehabilitation center. He's also a recovering alcoholic. His medical experience combined with his direct knowledge of alcoholism makes him one the best addiction specialists in the country. It was Dr. Fowler who taught me where my Sugar Demons came from.

As it turns out, all addiction, including sugar addiction, has everything to do with the chemical dopamine. Dopamine is the neurotransmitter our brain releases when it perceives we have done something good. It's an evolutionary mechanism that makes you feel good for doing that which is going to help you survive and produce offspring. This is what's known as a "reward pathway." For instance, a nourishing meal translates to a 30% increase in dopamine to let us know we have done a good thing by feeding our body a healthy meal. A glass of red wine translates to a 40-60% increase, unless you're an alcoholic, then it translates to a 300% increase in dopamine. Cocaine reliably translates to a 300% increase in all people, and crystal meth hits you with an 800% or higher increase in dopamine.

So you see how alcohol and other drugs can eventually rewire your brain into perceiving them as more important than food, sleep, or even the love of your family. If you've ever spent any amount of time around a junkie, the one thought constantly running through your head is, "Why can't you just stop?" Eventually you realize they can't. Their subconscious brain is too convinced the drug is intrinsic to survival, even if they're consciously aware that it's not. That's all addiction really is.

Sugar works on your brain the same way narcotics do. In fact, there are multiple studies showing sugar to be equally, if not more addictive than cocaine. Why is this? Imagine you live in a forest. The forest provides everything you need. You hunt for animals and gather fruits and veggies everyday for food. Life is mostly good until winter comes. In winter, the plants you're used to eating disappear, and much of the game goes into hibernation. Everyday becomes a struggle to get in enough calories for survival. This is how most humans actually lived until the advent of agriculture. Now imagine it's spring again. You're super skinny from experiencing near starvation over the winter. All of a sudden, food is growing on trees again. Most of it is sugar in the form of fruit. It's sweet and delicious. You gorge yourself on it for as long as you can. It replaces the fat you lost in winter, so you might survive the next winter. Sugar used to be crucial to our survival, that's why your brain releases dopamine every time you eat it. Pharmacologically, cocaine and sugar are different, but they both cause a similar dopamine increase in the brain. Repetitive use of sugar is how you create your very own Sugar Demons.

But if we can create Sugar Demons, why can't we create Broccoli Angels to help us fight them? Well, you can-sort of. As with all addiction, the key is finding a new habit to replace the bad habit. Most people start with exercise. It's a great place to start, but you can only exercise so many times per day and you're still going to get sugar cravings ALL THE TIME, even on days when you exercise. You have to find something you can rely on to fight the Sugar Demons every day. By trial and error, I came up with a list of foods I love to eat, instead of sugary/processed foods.

One of my Broccoli Angels is (wait for it) broccoli! I know it doesn't sound great, but it actually is. My coworker showed me how she drizzles coconut oil over her steamed broccoli. I tried it and fell in love. Coconut oil gives broccoli a subtle delicious sweetness, plus it's full of MCTs (medium chain triglycerides), which give you energy and train your metabolism to burn fat. Because broccoli and coconut oil are so nutrient dense, it tends to squash cravings for a good while. Broccoli Angels are perhaps the most crucial weapon in your arsenal to fight the Sugar Demons because, over time, they will replace all of the sugary/processed foods in your life.

Salted, dry roasted nuts are one of my Broccoli Angels. Bacon and eggs is an absolute lifesaver (and not just for breakfast). Lately, I've gotten really into sardines on Simple Mills grain-free crackers. I know some of my choices may sound really weird, but the point is you need to find your own Broccoli Angels, so you can turn to them whenever the Sugar Demons attack or, better yet, before they even get the chance.

Broccoli Angels are the opposite of Sugar Demons. They're the healthy foods we actually enjoy eating all the time. Experimenting and discovering healthy foods you enjoy is not only fun, it's also imperative to replace the old foods your Sugar Demons lead to. Without knowing your Broccoli Angels, you won't have a clue what to meal prep. In the next section of this chapter I will provide more examples of the Broccoli Angels I rely upon and some strategies for finding you own.

This book is my own version of a secret channel, showing you things other people don't want to see. It's a window into my sugar addiction, but maybe also a mirror to your own. Look at what I've faced. Learn from my failures. You can do this! You're much better prepared now then you were before reading this book.

Finding Angels

The first thing you must know about Broccoli Angels is they only work if you truly believe in them. Just kidding, they only work if you truly enjoy eating them. Broccoli Angels are the foods you choose to eat in place of your old diet. I purposely wrote this chapter after the chapter on meal prepping because I wanted you to see how fast and easy it is to make your own healthy, delicious food before going through the process of choosing a menu. Again, I cannot overstate this, Broccoli Angels must be foods you actually look forward to eating.

The second thing you need to remember about Broccoli Angels is they must be made up either entirely of green light foods, or mostly green light foods with a small, measured amount of foods from the yellow light category. In the examples below, I have Broccoli Angels that work for me divided into three categories: fat/protein, fat/low-carb, and safe-carb/protein.

Notice there are only two macro-nutrients present in each example. This serves two purposes:

1. It's easier to prep, making it easier to stay compliant with your diet.

2. Not eating carbs and fats together in the same meal speeds weight loss.

Finding your Broccoli Angels makes a great Superbetter quest! It's one that you will repeat multiple times as you become more comfortable in the kitchen and your cooking skills improve. There are a ton of resources out there to help you, but most people gravitate to Pinterest.com. Have fun scrolling!

Here are a few examples of fat/protein Broccoli Angels:

Bacon and eggs

Roasted chicken with guacamole or sliced avocado

Two tablespoons of Peanut or almond butter with your eggs (sounds weird, but try it)

Dry-roasted, salted nuts and a Stevia sweetened protein shake

Steak fajita meat dipped in melted grass-fed butter or ghee

A can of tuna mixed with an olive oil or avocado oil based mayo like Sir Kensington or Mark Sisson's Primal Kitchen Brand.

As you can see, all of these are a combination of healthy fats and proteins that are easy to keep around or carry with you for when the Sugar Demons come knocking.

Here are some examples of fat/low-carb options:

A bowl of steamed broccoli with melted coconut oil or olive oil drizzled over it. Easy peasy.

Any non-starchy vegetable dipped in grass fed-butter or ghee. For example, cauliflower would work, but carrots would not be as good a choice because of their carb content.

Any unsweetened almond butter on celery or other non-starchy vegetables.

Note: These options tend to make better snacks than they do meals.

Here are some examples of safe-carb/protein options:

Sweet potatoes and steak, chicken, pork, fish, or any healthy protein.

Canned sardines (this is a protein and a fat by itself) paired with one serving of Simple Mills crackers. More than one serving (about 12 crackers) is too carby, so be careful. Otherwise this is delicious and one of my absolute favorites!

Butternut squash spirals (buy pre-spiralized and frozen so you only have to defrost in the microwave) with sugar-free marinara and shrimp or whatever protein you have on hand.

Here's the good news, you can eat these foods whenever you like, in whatever quantities you like. With the exception of meals that contain yellow light foods, there's no need to worry about portion size. Just eat as much as you like until you're done. It's almost impossible to over eat these healthy foods. Unlike processed foods, that are designed to keep you eating by getting around your body's natural satiety signals, you're body will tell you when you've had enough Broccoli Angels.

Supplement Strategy #3

In order to explain this one, I have to drop some science knowledge on you. I promise to be brief, so we can get to the benefits of this amazing supplement.

Every cell in your body has an engine to power it. This engine is called the mitochondria. Your mitochondria can run on either glucose or ketones. Every carbohydrate you eat, whether it's sugar, bread, fructose, or sweet potato, gets converted into glucose. When glucose is present in significant quantities with regularity, your mitochondria will preferentially use it as fuel above all else. Fat loss is hard to come by in this scenario.

Ketones, on the other hand, are produced when your liver breaks down fatty acids into ketone molecules, which can also be used by your mitochondria for fuel. It does this when there's a lack of available glucose. In this scenario, your body is much more likely to break down stored fatty acids (the stuff on your thighs and mid-section) into fuel for your mitochondria. When your body is running on ketones, this is called being in ketosis.

Whether fat loss is a goal of yours or not, it's still desirable to be in ketosis at least sometimes. For one, most people report that it feels amazing. Energy and alertness improve without the jittery feeling you get from caffeine. For me, it's like switching over from gasoline to solar energy. The energy I have feels cleaner. Perhaps the most significant benefit of being in ketosis is that it decreases blood markers such as LDL cholesterol, triglycerides, and blood glucose, while increasing HDL cholesterol. Finally, hunger disappears to the point that it becomes easy to accidentally skip meals.

As stated earlier, I'm indifferent when it comes to how you choose to arrange your diet so long as you're not eating refined carbohydrates. You don't necessarily have to go low-carb in order to beat your Sugar Demons. That being said, unless you're purposely eating a lot of sweet potato and other starchy vegetables, most people are going to end up eating low-carb anyway. It's just easier to meal prep that way.

So what is MCT oil, and why should you use it?

MCT stands for Medium-Chain Triglyceride. It's a type of fat your body easily converts into energy but is also unlikely to store. Coconut oil is about 55 percent MCTs, which is why it can be substituted for MCT oil in a pinch or if MCT oil is too expensive for your budget. I recommend going with MCT oil, though, if you can afford it. Manufacturers of this supplement take MCTs from coconut and palm oil and concentrate them into pure 100 percent MCT oil. That's like turning dynamite into an atom bomb!

So let's get to why I recommend MCT oil as a supplement to aid your fight against the Sugar Demons. The ultimate goal for your metabolism is to achieve what's known as "metabolic flexibility" where your mitochondria can switch between burning glucose and ketones without any trouble at all. Unfortunately, if you've been eating refined carbs for a long time, your mitochondria will grudgingly switch to using ketones as fuel. It takes time for them to adapt to this new fuel source. This transition period can last a few days and it can produce flu-like symptoms otherwise known as "keto or low-carb flu".

Bear in mind that "keto flu" runs concurrently with the cravings and withdrawal symptoms you'll experience in the early days of quitting sugar. For most people, this is the most difficult time in their fight against the Sugar Demons. It's the time you are most vulnerable. Many people never make it out of this phase in the process, because giving in to their cravings is easier than suffering through withdrawal and "keto flu".

The longer you stay in the adaptation phase, the greater the risk of surrendering to your Sugar Demons. By supplementing with MCT oil, you'll increase your ketone levels before your body is producing them on it's own. It trains your mitochondria to adapt faster, thus shortening the time you experience sugar withdrawal, which is physically the most difficult part of this process. In other words, it gets you to the "promised land" faster and with less bumps along the way. An added benefit is once your metabolism is fat adapted, sugar cravings tend to decrease as well. Anything that shortens or eliminates "keto flu" *and* sugar cravings is a powerful weapon against the Sugar Demons.

MCT oil might be the Excalibur of demon slayers, and here's how I use it. I use MCT oil every day in my coffee. It's flavorless, but gives my coffee that creamy texture most people use dairy to achieve. This is a supplement you want to start small with. I use a tablespoon but recommend starting with a teaspoon as MCTs can cause loose stools if you over do it. You can gradually increase your dose or just go for it and deal with the consequences for a few days until your stomach adapts. If you're not a coffee drinker, you can add it to salads or other foods. You won't even notice it's there. Also, there's nothing wrong with just downing a spoonful plain. It's flavorless, so you won't have to hold your nose or anything.

Chapter Four Cheat Sheet

- Broccoli Angels are healthy, sugar-free, unprocessed foods you actually enjoy eating.
- **If your diet does not consist of foods you actually like to eat, then it is not sustainable and you will eventually succumb to your Sugar Demons. Any dietary advice to the contrary is either a fad, or someone trying to sell you something useless.**
- Try to enjoy the process of discovering your Broccoli Angels. Make it a quest. Use google and Pintrest.com for ideas.
- MCT oil can speed your transition from a carbohydrate based metabolism to a metabolically flexible metabolism that can easily switch between burning carbs for energy and burning fat for energy.
- MCT oil helps you fight the Sugar Demons by lessening the adaptation phase (keto flu) and getting you into the "promised land" faster.

Chapter 5
Changing Your Cage

There were other addictions beside sugar. Cigarettes became a part of my life around age twelve. It sort of came with being an accepted member of the skater/smoker crowd at my school, the ones who wore graphic tees and Airwalk shoes before they went mainstream. My own vanity helped me break that addiction. It turns out it's hard to get really buff when you're a smoker. The cigarettes don't leave you with enough appetite to support any extra muscle. At the wise old age of seventeen, I'd decided it was in my best interest to fill out my clothes a little more and finally grow a butt that was worth being checked out by the ladies so I replaced smoking with more gym time and a larger appetite for protein shakes. I'm making it sound easy, but it wasn't.

After high school, I graduated to diet pills with scary-cool names like Lypodrine, Xenadrine, Hydroxycut, and Ripped Fuel. We call them ECA stacks because all of them contain the same three basic ingredients: ephedrine, caffeine, and aspirin. They work, because the combination of those ingredients artificially increases your metabolism. Of course, they're illegal now due to the ephedrine. Too many criminals were buying ephedrine products to cook meth. In the late 90's and early 2000's, you had these guys going into stores buying as many bottles of diet pills and cough medicines as the stores could keep in stock. Eventually, people caught on, and stores selling ephedrine-containing products began limiting customers to one or two products per customer. The criminals responded by shopping multiple store locations until they could accumulate enough product to cook a batch of meth. "Smurphing" is the street term for shopping around like this for ephedrine.

Some of pills I used to take still exist under the same brand name, but the formulas are all different now. Mind you, I wasn't taking diet pills to lose weight. I just preferred them to ADHD medications. They helped me focus in college and allowed me to work late nights as a bartender. I got so used to taking them that sometimes I would wash down three or four pills with a sugar-free Red Bull just before my shift. Some nights, I'd wake up with my heart beating so hard it shook the bed.

My first panic attack occurred at 29, approximately ten years after my dependence on the diet pills began. After some quick research to confirm my own suspicions, I stopped taking the pills. Cold turkey. Apparently if you abuse caffeine in excess of 200 milligrams per day, you're way more likely to develop panic disorder. Between the energy drinks and the pills, I'd been taking in over a thousand milligrams of caffeine a day for ten years!

I anticipated my first caffeine-free bar tending shift to be a nightmare, but it wasn't. Even though the shift lasted until 4 a.m., I had no problem staying alert. There were other withdrawal symptoms, though. What can only be described as an "ice pick" headache was my constant companion that night behind the bar, but my lack of exhaustion perplexed me. That is until I realized the benefits of the caffeine stopped working for me long before I'd stopped taking it. I didn't need caffeine to work a late shift anymore, because it hadn't been helping me do that anyway. I just kept taking it past it's usefulness because I liked the feeling it gave me. After that realization, I didn't touch caffeine again for a very long time.

Though they're illegal to sell as one product, you can make your own ECA stacks by combining multiple over-the-counter products. It's really simple. I know this, because at forty I decided to do a bodybuilding competition. For accelerated fat loss my coaches advised me to take a combo of Vivarin (caffeine), baby aspirin, and Bronch-Aid (ephedrine) before my morning cardio sessions. That's how you make your own ECA stack. I did it once, but it made me feel dead inside to the point I wasn't enjoying my workout anymore. Maybe it's what I needed to get through college but not anymore. I stuck with just a small dose of caffeine before hitting the treadmill after that.

Meanwhile, my sugar addiction was always close by. It didn't start before or after my other addictions, it ran concurrently with them. All through my twenties and thirties, I used it to cope with life's little stressors the same way I used the diet pills and the cigarettes before that. You might think I have an addictive personality, but don't we all? Isn't the psychological side of addiction just feeling like you need something to cope? A little ritual to help you deal with the psychic pain of living a modern life? Many of my CrossFit friends punish themselves in the gym daily and will give up fast food for a healthier diet but still can't manage to part with that glass of wine at the end of the work day. We all cope.

The point is, we all have our own addictions for our own reasons. We believe it's the physical part of addiction that's so dangerous and difficult to cure, but it's not. It's the psychological component that gets us. The physical symptoms of sugar withdrawal will pass within a few weeks at most, but the psychological symptoms are what cause us to relapse. Those who read my blog know the "promised land" is my nickname for when I make it through those first ten days without sugar where the cravings and other physical symptoms of my disease disappear. Life gets much easier for me once I'm there. But I can't count how many times I've been to the "promised land" only to relapse because of something as trivial as a schedule change or a bad day at work. How do we win the psychological side of this war?

Lately, I've been reading *Chasing The Scream* by Johann Hari. It's about the drug war, and how we view addiction. I agree with him that all our perceptions of addiction are flawed. In his book Johann talks about how the old experiments with rats in cages misled us into our current understanding of addiction. We used to put rats in cages with two water drips to choose from. One contained only water, the other contained water laced with cocaine. Predictably, the rats would addict themselves to the cocaine drip and eventually overdose. This is how we began to understand addiction as a physical need we bring upon ourselves.

But there are newer experiments that contradict this theory. When you run the same experiment in a rat park (a really fun environment for rats) versus a cage, they hardly touch the cocaine drip. Even if you put cocaine-addicted rats into the rat park, they will quickly ween themselves off the cocaine drip. It's not the presence of cocaine that makes these rats into addicts, it's the cage.

To run a similar experiment on humans would be criminally irresponsible, but it's already been done. We called it the Vietnam war. According to Johann (and *Time* magazine), around 20 percent of service members in Vietnam became addicted to heroine during their deployment. It was such a widespread problem that politicians of the time warned of crime and the coming health crisis when all these "junkies" returned from the war. It never materialized. Only about 5 percent of soldiers kept using heroine, the same number that would have probably become drug addicts anyway.

War is a terrible cage to live in. In Vietnam, heroine was a way for our troops to cope with it. Once our soldiers were out of that situation, they no longer needed the heroine to get by. Similar to the rat experiments, they came home to a better cage. In order to be successful against sugar addiction in the long term, you have to learn how to change your cage. In the next section, I will teach you how to do that.

A.I.M.

Let's talk about the rat park for a moment. I was purposely vague on the details of what a rat park is in the last section, only to assert that it's better than a cage, because I'd like to go over it in detail right here. What are the differences between a rat park and a cage? Why is it better?

When you to visit a rat park, the first thing you'll notice is that it's considerably larger than a rat cage. It has lots of room for the rats to chase each other around. The other thing you will immediately notice is that it's not a cage at all. It's more of an L-shaped wooden box with a forest mural painted on the inside to mimic a more natural environment. There are empty soup cans and other obstacles for the rats to climb on or hide in. Perhaps most important, there are plenty of other rats to socialize with.

The rat park attempts to mimic, as much as possible, the natural environment of a rat. It's not a prefect reconstruction by any means, but it's a vast improvement over wire cages with wood chip floors. Applying the rat cage versus rat park metaphor to ourselves provides significant clues as to how we can live in a way that enables us to be successful against our Sugar Demons in the long term. It tells us how to change our cage from a prison into a park.

If you're an average American like myself, you might be thinking, "Great, all I need to do is spend lots of money (that I don't have) to improve my surroundings so I don't give in to my Sugar Demons." Don't fret! You can do all of this stuff without spending any money. Admittedly, a few of my recommendations involve spending small amounts of money, but only for the sake of convenience, and I offer free alternatives to each of them. The most important thing to keep in mind about all of this is that we are fighting addiction. It may not be heroine addiction, but it *is* addiction nonetheless. You must have a plan of attack.

Using the rat park as a model, I've isolated what I believe to be the three most important areas of your life to focus on when it comes to changing your cage and turned them into an acronym. These areas are Activity, Isolation Avoidance, and Mindfullness, or **A.I.M.** for short. Not everyone will need to focus on all three areas at once. Some of you may already be excelling in one or two areas. In that case, just focus on improving the other areas you're weak in. Let's look at all three parts of A.I.M. in detail.

Activity

The biggest, most obvious difference between a rat cage and a rat park is the rat park has way more stuff to do. As humans, our minds and bodies crave stimulus. Without it, we fall into boredom. Bored people learn to go right to their coping mechanism the way caged rats learn to go right to the cocaine drip. This is especially important to pay attention to on weekends and holidays. You might assume having lots of time on your hands to lie on the couch and watch Netflix is good, especially after a long work week, but it can be a recipe for disaster.

Think about it. When you sit on the couch to watch a show, you're already conditioned from years of poor eating habits to grab something to snack on. Even if it's not a sugary snack initially, that sort of mindless eating can lead you down the slippery slope to worse and worse food choices. I can remember plenty of times where I started the day snacking on roasted almonds and finished the day with my face in a bowl of ice cream. This occurs because when you turn off the active parts of your brain to passively watch television, the limbic system (lizard brain), all impulses and desires, becomes primarily active. With other parts of the brain relegated to the background, you don't have as much cognitive restraint over these impulses. That's how you end up going from couch to cupboard without realizing how you got there.

Avoiding this situation requires a little planning. You must take control of your down time. I'm not saying you can't watch TV anymore, but it shouldn't be the only thing on your agenda. Try to fill your weekends with three or four activities to be done before collapsing on the couch to enjoy passive activities like watching TV or playing video games. It doesn't really matter what activities you choose so long as you enjoy doing them. They can be simple things like iPhone photography, hiking in your neighborhood, or a DIY project around the house. Now would be a great time to find a hobby if you don't already have one. If you get stuck coming up with things to do, Pinterest is a fantastic resource.

It's crucial that you go into the weekend with a plan, instead of just letting the weekend happen to you. Here's an example of how I fill my weekends, broken down into morning and afternoon activities.

Saturday AM:

> Write for at least an hour while I sip my coffee.

> Take my dog to the park. While my dog is busy playing, I'll use my phone to quest for Broccoli Angels and plan my grocery for the week.

> Grocery Shopping.

> Read a book or find something relevant to share on my Sugar Demons Facebook group.

Saturday PM:

> Gym/CrossFit

> Yoga or meditation (mindfulness activity) in the living room.

Sundays are basically the same as Saturday except instead of going to the gym I meal prep.

As you can see, I tend toward more physical activities, but you don't have to. Just be sure to fill your off days with stuff that interests you. Once you've checked off a few activities it's perfectly okay to chill on the couch for awhile. Remember to always be cognizant of your lizard brain. The Sugar Demons live there and they're guaranteed to send you some strong impulses. It's not a bad idea to take some L-glutamine beforehand to head off those cravings. Next, we'll take a look at the second part of A.I.M., Isolation Avoidance.

Isolation Avoidance

Being an introvert, this tends to be the area of my life I have to put the most effort into. But forget about me for a moment, let's go back to the rat park. Perhaps the most important difference between the park and the cage is that the park is home to several rats while the cage holds only one. Without other rats to connect with, the isolated rats will overdose 100 percent of the time. Similar to rats, humans are social creatures. Our bodies crave connection just as much as they crave stimulus. Johann Hari once said in a TED Talk, "The opposite of addiction is not sobriety. The opposite of addiction is connection." Speaking from my own experience, social isolation is the perfect environment for a relapse.

It's easy to isolate one's self. As a proud introvert, I used to think I didn't crave human connection like other people. Turns out, my body just craves it in a different way. It took being married for several years before I figured this out. It's a running joke in our household that it takes exactly 72 hours for me to miss my wife. Like all good jokes, there's a measure of truth to this. What I mean is that it takes 72 hours of isolation for me to experience feelings of loneliness. This doesn't mean going long periods of time without human interaction is healthy for me. It's not.

What took me a while to notice is that when my wife is away, it only takes 24 hours before my cravings begin to increase in frequency. They don't necessarily get stronger, only eating refined carbohydrates causes that, but the time in between cravings shortens dramatically. When I'm isolated, I tend to either relapse or inch towards it by eating more yellow-light foods than I should. While as an introvert, I would love nothing more than to sequester myself inside the house with my Xbox and a few good books, but I now know this is not a good plan for me.

Now, when my wife goes out of town, I make sure to schedule some time with friends. I also force myself to say "Yes" to more social situations in general. CrossFit has been absolutely critical for my social life. Every CrossFit gym is its own little community of fitness enthusiasts, but even when we travel, I find it easy to connect with the people I meet in other CrossFit gyms around the world. It doesn't matter if your community is a church, a volunteer group, or a group exercise class; being part of a community is super important when looking to avoid isolation.

Below I've listed some suggestions for avoiding isolation. Google, Facebook groups, and Pinterest can also be a great resource for finding social activities.

My list of strategies to combat isolation:

Become a member of a church or spiritual group. Not only will you gain a community, but these communities tend to put on lots of social events.

Join a group fitness class like CrossFit, Zumba, or Soul Cycle. If these are out of your budget, check out some running clubs. These are groups of people who plan weekly runs together. Running is free and good for you!

Volunteer! The range of possibilities here is exciting: hospital, retirement home, prison, animal shelter; whatever you're into, there's a place that needs your help. Not only will you bond with the people/animals you're there to help, but you might make lifelong friends with other volunteers.

Join a book club. This one is perfect for introverts. What self-respecting introvert doesn't want to read a book and then discuss what they internalized with other people? Check the Internet or your local library for posted groups.

Being isolated doesn't make me sad as it does some people. In fact, I crave isolation. Gaining energy from "alone time" is part of what it means to be an introvert. That being said, without people to ground me, I lose sight of my reasons for wanting to avoid sugar and stay healthy in the first place. If anything I'm saying speaks to you at all, make avoiding isolation a part of your plan ASAP. In the long term fight against the Sugar Demons, it might just save your life.

Now, let's take a look at the final part of A.I.M., Mindfulness.

Mindfulness

While mindfulness might be the most annoying buzzword of 2018, it's also the key to living a balanced life. Since it's not physically observable, we don't have to revisit the rat park to understand this one. We need only to understand the nature of animals. Unlike humans, animals spend the majority of their time living in the moment. The further you get down the food chain, the more true this becomes. Rats and other animals are killing it in the mindfulness department because they're not burdened with thoughts about the past or the future. They don't dwell on things the way humans do.

Being present in the moment is all mindfulness really is. Modern humans are terrible at this. We're always thinking about trivial things, like the person who was rude to us the day before or what might go wrong at work tomorrow. It stops us from enjoying the life we're living right now. It also makes us weak-minded.

If you're sometimes bombarded by unwanted thoughts and find it difficult to turn them off, it's because you've never exercised the part of your brain that does that. Spending time purposely focusing on your breath while watching your thoughts go by until they stop is what is called "practicing" mindfulness. In other words, you can train yourself to be in the moment, instead of thinking about stuff while the moment passes you by.

As modern humans, we're always impatiently jumping from the thing holding our attention right now, to the next thing that will. Without mindfulness to ground us in the present, our minds are constantly in "seeking mode." In "seeking mode," our state of mind is permanently on the lookout for the next news article, social media post, movie, book, lover, drug, or meal that will recapture our attention; until it doesn't, and we're off seeking the next thing that will. The Sugar Demons are always ready to be that next thing. Regaining our ability to be present is the key to increasing the pleasures we get out of life and a defensive fortification against the Sugar Demon's attempts at robbing us of our happiness.

While living in the moment leads to better appreciation of everyday life, another equally important benefit to practicing mindfulness is that it gives you more executive control over your thoughts. Remember how the limbic system (your lizard brain) is responsible for survival instincts and rewarding behaviors? Well, the frontal and prefrontal cortex are responsible for executive function. When we practice mindfulness it strengthens our frontal/prefrontal cortex, thus improving executive function. Executive function governs some very non-lizard-brain functions such as attention, impulse control, working memory, cognitive flexibility, and emotional regulation. The two traits that stand out to me the most from that list are impulse control and emotional regulation.

As stated in chapter three, I don't rely solely on willpower to defeat my Sugar Demons because I know it doesn't work. That being said, having stronger impulse control and emotional regulation equates to more willpower. Though it's likely not enough by itself to cure your addiction, a measure of willpower is still necessary to win this war. It still requires some willpower to choose your home-prepped lunch over the free pizza in the break room or to make the choice to stay sugar-free when circumstances beyond your control put you in a difficult food environment.

Here are some resources to help you begin practicing mindfulness:

The website www.mindful.org. This is a free resource, containing everything you need to establish a mindfulness practice. This is really all you need, but I also use the next two paid resources, because they are convenient and tend to hold my attention better than just practicing on my own.

Headspace. Headspace is a paid app where an actual Buddhist monk guides you through 10 minute meditations. As you progress through the app, it gives you the option to increase the length of your practice. I find this app to be invaluable. The subscription is less than $15 dollars per month.

ROMWOD. ROMWOD, which stands for Range Of Motion Workout Of The Day is another fairly inexpensive subscription service that provides daily 20 minute Yoga routines. As a professed hater of Yoga, I actually don't mind doing this one. It doesn't require a mat, and you don't have to take your shoes off. The poses are more relaxing than challenging, and there's a voice that guides you through everything including breath work. As a CrossFit athlete I find ROMWOD to be a nice way of getting in some post-workout stretching while also practicing being mindful. It's only 20 minutes a day, which makes it easy to establish a daily routine.

Putting A.I.M. into practice

In addition to everything else in this book, A.I.M. is a lot to work on. Don't panic! A.I.M. fits nicely into the framework of Superbetter. In the final chapter of this book, I provide you with a step-by-step plan for putting everything together into one cohesive strategy.

Supplement Strategy #4

My first foray into magnesium supplementation was a disaster. Without doing proper research, I chose a product that contains higher-than-normal levels of arsenic. Lesson learned. When choosing a supplement, even a basic mineral supplement like magnesium, one can never be too careful. Heavy-metal poisoning is less than desirable. Fortunately, I switched brands before any real damage was done. At least, that's what I tell myself. Now, when purchasing a supplement, I use the website labdoor.com to check it out first. They lab test a ton of supplements on the market and generate detailed reports on each. Plus, they have an A through F grading system, it's easy to determine if a particular supplement is worth throwing your money at. Even if I don't buy a supplement directly from labdoor.com (they usually redirect you to Amazon anyway), I always use the Web site to check it out first.

Okay, so why magnesium? Well, a quick Google search will bring up about a hundred pages of articles, most telling you the same thing: We are all deficient in magnesium. There are numerous reasons for this. Depleted soil, fluoride in our water, alcohol consumption; all of these either keep us from getting enough magnesium or rob us of the magnesium we already have. However, the most damaging to our efforts of getting and keeping up adequate levels of magnesium is sugar. Apparently, each molecule of sugar we consume requires twenty-eight molecules of magnesium to metabolize properly. That's a pretty high price to pay, biochemically speaking!

So what does magnesium actually do? A better question might be: What doesn't it do? Magnesium is involved in over three hundred different functions in the body including bone health, calcium absorption, sleep, regulating cholesterol levels, circulation, vitamin D absorption, digestion, and the list goes on. Basically, being magnesium deficient puts a strain on every major system of the body. Just being magnesium deficient can lead to an increase in sugar cravings, but my reason for recommending it here is for its impact on sleep.

Nothing will set off sugar cravings like a poor night's sleep. It's like putting your Sugar Demons on steroids. Proper sleep hygiene can help with this, but a nice hit of magnesium before bedtime can really improve the quality of your slumber. Really, magnesium is more of a sleep supplement, and a good night's sleep is what will help protect you from the Sugar Demons. What I love about magnesium is you can actually feel it working. You feel your body begin to relax making it easier to fall asleep. Once asleep, magnesium keeps you in the deep, restorative stages of sleep longer.

Once you try it, you'll see what I mean. Magnesium is fantastic for sleep! That being said, I must caution you not to rely solely on magnesium for a good night's rest. Proper sleep hygiene is still the most effective way to ensure quality sleep. Magnesium should only be a supplement to this, not a replacement. Here is what proper sleep hygiene looks like:

- Sleep in total darkness if possible.
- Go to bed at the same time every night.
- Turn off all screens about an hour before bed. This includes laptops, cell phones, and televisions.
- Dim the lights an hour before going to bed.
- Take your magnesium about half an hour prior to getting into bed.

Currently I'm using Life Extension Magnesium Caps for my nightly ritual. It contains magnesium citrate, magnesium succinate, and magnesium oxide. Citrate tends to be the best for absorption, so be sure to shop for a magnesium supplement that has it.

One final note: magnesium can act as a laxative if you take too much, so start with a low dose and work your way up to the full recommended dose.

Chapter Five Cheat Sheet

- Once you reach the "Promised Land" you enter the second phase of the fight against your Sugar Demons, keeping them from creeping back into your life by employing A.I.M..
- A.I.M. stands for Activity, Isolation Avoidance, and Mindfulness.
- Use A.I.M to bring balance to your life so the Sugar Demons don't have a doorway back in.
- **Quality of sleep is extremely important in dealing with sugar addiction. A poor nights sleep will leave you vulnerable to the Sugar Demons.**
- Practicing good sleep hygiene and incorporating a Magnesium supplement can go a long way toward improving sleep quality and overall health.

Chapter 6
Putting it All Together

This final chapter is a series of quests to help you put together all of the strategies in this book. Think of it as your battle plan. These quests are in logical order, but feel free to add in your own quests along the way as you see fit. You can go through these at your own speed as long as you're completing at least one quest everyday. As long as you keep moving forward, you'll eventually build enough momentum to steam roll the Sugar Demons, so they never gain a foothold in your life again.

Good luck!

Quest #1

Find your secret identity.

List three qualities you'll need to defeat your Sugar Demons. Examples: determination, willpower, courage

1. _____

2. _____

3. _____

Now list three of your favorite characters who embody these characteristics.

Feel free to choose any character you can think of from books, movies, TV, etcetera.

1. _____

2. _____

3. _____

Finally, choose the character who appeals to you the most and combine that character's name with your own in any way you like. Examples: Jedi Johnathan, Sonya the Sugar Demon Slayer, Captain Joemerica.

Put the final result down on paper right here:

I am now _____.

Quest #2

Create a list of power ups you can use daily.

I've started it for you. Add as many as you can think of right now, and don't be afraid to come back to add more to the list as you discover what works for you. Remember, a power up is anything physical, emotional, or social that gives you a quick burst of positive energy.

1. Do something physical! Examples: Do ten squats at your desk, go for a run/walk, hit the gym.

2. Take a supplement. Yep, supplements can double as power ups!

3. Hug a pet, friend, or family member. Not a hugger? High five someone.

4. _____

5. _____

6. _____

7. _____

8. _____

9. _____

10. _____

11. _____

12. _____

13. _____

14. _____

15. _____

Quest #3

Get sugar and refined carbohydrates out of the house.

Step 1.

Get a garbage bag.

Step 2.

Look at the stuff in your refrigerator and pantry. Anything that comes in a box or plastic container probably needs to go. Just to be sure, look at the ingredients. If anything from the list I provided in chapter one is in there, It. Has. To. Go.

Step 3.

Fill your garbage bag. If you completely fill one bag and still have more processed foods in your house simply repeat steps one through three until it is all gone.

Did you do it? Sign your secret identity name right here:

I did it! _____

Don't sign unless you actually did it.

Quite an eye opening experience wasn't it? Circle: Yes No

Quest #4

Start taking control of your food environment.

Today's quest is about preparing for something many people are afraid of; your first meal prep. Don't panic! The actual Meal prep is still two quests away. This quest is just to make sure you have everything you need to complete the meal prep quest.

Step 1.

Check out your kitchen. Do you have everything you need to meal prep and keep your food environment with you? I'm going to assume you already have a microwave and stove top oven.

Circle any of the following items if they are missing from your kitchen:

Twelve-to-fifteen inch frying pan

Five-quart pot (if you plan to boil eggs)

Spatula

Roasting pan

Aluminum foil

A lunch box

Cold inserts for the lunch box

A food scale to measure out portions

Glass or plastic containers (to transport your food in)

Paper towels (for the mess)

Step 2. Go out and buy the stuff you're missing. You can also order this stuff from Amazon or just go to www.thesugardemons.com where it's all conveniently in one place.

Did you do it? Sign your secret identity name here:

I did it! _____

Quest #5

Find your Broccoli Angels

Finding your own Broccoli Angels is a highly individual thing based upon your own personal preferences for food. Personally, I love a good can of sardines but I know I'm in the minority on this one. To help you come up with your own angels I've designed this quest. Keep in mind that the only requirements for something to be a Broccoli Angel is that it's sugar-free, unprocessed, nutrient rich, and you love eating it.

Let's pic an easy one first. Go back to the list of green-light carbs in chapter one. Out of the starchy or non-starchy vegetables listed, choose the two or three you like the most and list them here:

1. _____

2. _____

3. _____

Okay, now just pair with any protein from the green-light list of proteins and you got a meal!

Choose one or two and write down the combination. Example: Steak and sweet potato, chicken and broccoli, pork steaks and butternut squash.

Write down what you came up with:

Broccoli Angel #1

_____

Okay, now let's try to find a different kind of Broccoli Angel, a protein and healthy fat combo.

Take any protein, so long as it's not highly processed (high quality sausage is fine, but not lunch meat), and pair it with a healthy fat.

Example: Applegate Sausage and avocado, eggs and bacon, a can of tuna fish stirred up in some Primal Kitchen Mayo.

Broccoli Angel #2

Congratulations! Now you have two Broccoli Angels to prep for this week. Now go out and buy the ingredients.

Quest #6

Meal Prep

Just relax okay? Even if you mess this up, you'll learn something. It's going to take about an hour (not including grocery shopping), so make sure to set aside at least that much time before starting this quest. Also, it's totally fine if you want to split this quest up into two days; one for grocery, and one for actually cooking.

Step 1.

Decide what you're going to prep for the week. Refer back to chapter three "Meal Prep in Under an Hour".

Step 2.

Make a list of all the things you need to get from the grocery store to meal prep.

Step 3.

Go buy all those delicious sugar-free ingredients!

Step 4.

Cook the food.

Step 5.

Store your food in the refrigerator in little glass or plastic food containers.

Remember to put your cold inserts in the freezer, so they're ready the next day to put in your lunch box, so your food keeps fresh until it's lunchtime.

Did you do it? Sign your secret identity name here:

I did it! _____

Awesome! You're really on your way now. Make this a weekly habit, so you're always in control of your food environment.

Quest #7

Define Your Epic Win

This one is simple. We just need to set a goal. How ambitious are you feeling? Whatever you come up with, it needs to be a real challenge. Think you can make it to the promised land? That's a good place to start for most people. If making it to the promised land sounds too easy, try setting a time domain. "I will make it through the holidays, November through December, without a relapse" is a bit more ambitious. Think you can make it an entire year without a relapse? Go for it!

Remember, set a goal that is possible, but has a real chance of failure. It's not an Epic Win if you don't have to strive for it. Also, remember that if you fail, just reflect on what you learned and set a new goal. Sugar addiction is one of the most difficult addictions to shake, and relapses are likely along the way. As long as you keep setting goals, learning from your mistakes, and fighting to save your own life, you will conquer your Sugar Demons.

Write down your Epic Win:

_____

_____

_____

Switching over to A.I.M.

The first seven quests should really help to get you through to the "promised land". Just keep playing Superbetter every day with the power ups we came up with, and you'll get there. Once you've completed the first seven quests, it's time to start switching our quests to focus more on the A.I.M. principles from chapter five. The next four quests will help you put A.I.M. into practice. Just don't neglect your daily power ups and weekly meal prep.

Quest #8

Activity: Planning for Down Time

You already know that having too much down time is a recipe for disaster. Whether you're in the "promised land" or still struggling in the early days of abstaining from sugar, not filling your free time with constructive activities can lead directly to relapse.

Let's set a plan for your next weekend or holiday. Choose at least three activities to fill your days with so you don't spend all of it on the couch. If you don't know what you like to do, try researching hobbies/activities on Google or Pinterest. Grocery shopping, meal prep, and gym time are totally fine to use, but try to come up with a few others.

List three activities for Saturday:

1. _____

2. _____

3. _____

List three activities for Sunday:

1. _____

2. _____

3. _____

Staying busy should act as a bulwark against the Sugar Demons. Stay the course. You're on your way to victory!

Quest #9

Recruit an Ally

Recruiting allies to help you achieve your goals is a big part of the game Superbetter, but it also doubles as a strategy for Isolation Avoidance, which is the "I" in A.I.M. Getting someone to help you find power ups and design quests for you can really boost your game. It also comes with the added benefit of bringing you closer to that person. By recruiting them as an ally, you're giving them the opportunity to play an active role in your recovery. Nothing strengthens bonds between people like giving and receiving help.

Step 1. Contact a friend or family member you trust to help you fight the Sugar Demons. You may reveal your secret identity to them if you're feeling really comfortable.

Step 2. Explain the rules of Superbetter to them. Have them send you one new quest per week or two new ideas for power ups.

Step 3. That's it.

Did you do it? Sign your secret identity name here:

I did it! _____

Wow, you're getting really strong, even if you don't know it yet. Are the Sugar Demons starting to go quiet? If not, just hang in there. It'll happen soon.

Quest #10

Join a Community

It doesn't matter if your community is a church, a volunteer group, or a group exercise class as long as you feel connected to the people of that community. If you're already part of a community, try taking a more active role. Volunteer to provide a service for the group or take on an office like treasurer. The more involved you are, the less isolated you'll be. Also, be sure to join our Facebook group: *Sugar Addiction: Kill the Sugar Demons!* Bear in mind though, online communities are no where near as effective as communities that meet in real life, so you still have to join a "real" community to complete this quest. If you get stuck, refer back to chapter five for ideas.

Did you do it? Sign your secret identity name here:

I did it! _____

Great! You're almost to the end now. One last quest, and we're done!

Quest #11

Begin a mindfulness practice (meditation, Yoga, ROMWOD, Wim Hof)

The final quest is to begin practicing mindfulness. The best way to do this is to set aside a few minutes each day to practice whatever version of mindfulness appeals to you. You might choose to join a Yoga studio, which conveniently doubles as a community, or you might choose to practice by yourself at home in your living room with the ROMWOD app. Silent meditation is a great free option as well. If you have some extra money, the Headspace app is a great way to develop mindfulness through guided meditations. Up for a real mindfulness challenge? Wim Hof breathing is another way to practice mindfulness while developing resilience to extreme cold. Whatever you decide to do, the most important thing is to make it a daily habit.

Step 1. Explore the different mindfulness options I've mentioned here and in chapter five.

Step 2. Choose the one that resonates with you.

Step 3. Start today.

Did you do it? Sign your secret identity name here:

I did it! _____

Congratulations! You've completed all my quests. Now keep playing by completing your own (and your allies) quests every day until you're back in total control of your life. Don't forget to activate those power ups, too.

#

Thank you for reading The Sugar Demons! I wish you well on your journey to freedom from all of your addictions and anything else that stands in the way of you living your best life. For the sake of convenience, all the supplements and other products mentioned in this book can be purchased on Amazon.com and may be found in one spot at the link below. Plus bonus content!

www.thesugardemons.com

Printed in Great Britain
by Amazon

19518241R00068